D0931492

THE
VALUE
EFFECT

THE VALUE EFFECT

A Murder Mystery about the Compulsive Pursuit of "The Next Big Thing"

John Guaspari

BK

BERRETT-KOEHLER PUBLISHERS, INC.
San Francisco

Berrett-Koehler Publishers, Inc.
450 Sansome Street, Suite 1200
San Francisco, CA 94111-3320
Tel: (415) 288-0260   Fax: (415) 362-2512   www.bkconnection.com

ORDERING INFORMATION

Quantity sales. Special discounts are available on quantity purchases by corporations, associations, and others. For details, contact the "Special Sales Department" at the Berrett-Koehler address above.

Individual sales. Berrett-Koehler publications are available through most bookstores. They can also be ordered direct from Berrett-Koehler:
Tel: (800) 929-2929; Fax: (802) 864-7626; www.bkconnection.com

Orders for college textbook/course adoption use.
Please contact Berrett-Koehler:
Tel: (800) 929-2929; Fax: (802) 864-7626.

Orders by U.S. trade bookstores and wholesalers.
Please contact Publishers Group West, 1700 Fourth Street, Berkeley, CA 94710.
Tel: (510) 528-1444; Fax (510) 528-3444.

Printed in the United States of America

Printed on acid-free and recycled paper that is composed of 85% recovered fiber, including 15% post-consumer waste.

Library of Congress Cataloging-in-Publication Data
Guaspari, John
    The value effect : a murder mystery about the complulsive pursuit of "the next big thing" / by John Guaspari. — 1st ed.
        p. cm.
    ISBN 1-57675-092-2 (acid-free paper)
    1. Customer relations—Fiction. 2. Executives—Fiction. I Title.

PS3557.U233 V3 2000
813'.54—DC21

00-260263

First Edition
    05   04   03   02   01   00   10 9 8 7 6 5 4 3 2 1

For Veronica

Acknowledgements

It is axiomatic in the consulting business that real learning occurs out in the real world with one's clients, not alone in an office with one's thoughts. So it would be an oversight (if not downright hypocritical) to have written a book about the singular power of customer value without acknowledging the value of my customers. Over the past fifteen years, I have had the opportunity to work with thousands of clients, in hundreds of client organizations, in scores of industries. That experience has been, to put it mildly, valuable. I hope that I was able to deliver something approaching equal value to them in the process.

National Grange Mutual Insurance Company, of Keene, New Hampshire, was my primary client in 1998; I learned more about the Value Effect during 1998 than I had in my previous forty-seven years on the planet; this was not a coincidence. My thanks especially to, in alphabetical order: Larry Acord, Steve Canty, Susan Hay, Phil Koerner, Judge Parker, and Tom Van Berkel.

From 1990–95, I worked for Rath & Strong (now a division of Aon Consulting).* Over those five years, I learned much from my R&S colleagues, and I value my continuing association with Dan Quinn and his staff. In particular, I am grateful to have had the chance to spend many, many hours kicking around "all this value stuff" with Bill Band (now with KPMG) and Tom Thomson. I hope they feel the same way.

*A few, very brief passages from the final section of this book ("The Evidence") were based on: (1) material appearing in the leader's guide to the training video "The Force of Value"; and (2) papers or articles written while the author was an employee of Rath & Strong Management Consultants. These passages appear in this book with the written permission of CRM Films, L.P., and Rath & Strong/Aon Consulting, respectively.

As these words are written, my second three-year term on the board of directors of the Association for Quality and Participation is drawing to a close. (I can't run again: term limits.) I have gained much from my association with AQP, personally as well as professionally. It is an organization that is right in the thick of the how-can-we-tap-into-the-full-potential-of-all-of-our-people fray. They do good work. They are headquartered in Cincinnati. Their Web site is at *www.aqp.org*. You owe it to yourself to check it out.

Not only did Mike Snell, my agent, bring Berrett-Koehler and me together, but he also provided useful editorial advice and feedback, for which I am in his debt. (Aside to Mike: that part about being "in debt" is just a figure of speech.)

Bob Anderson was once my boss, is still my friend. His commentary on an early draft of this book was, as always, extraordinarily insightful.

Readers of Berrett-Koehler publications already know Peter Block. I can attest to the fact that Peter is, to use the technical term, the real deal. His feedback and counsel (sometimes painful to hear, always worthwhile) were given as both business associate and friend. That's not an easy thing to pull off. He did it masterfully.

I first started talking to Steve Piersanti about "a value book" in the summer of 1997. It has taken three years to make it happen. It's felt like a lot longer than that. That's because Steve wouldn't let me off the hook. He kept pushing. Demanding. Not giving me an easy way out. In the process, he was doing what a good editor does; he was making it a better book. If you find its contents helpful, you can thank Steve. (If not, blame me.)

Nort Salz is my business partner. Nort's normal mode is this: "Come on! Let's go! Let's take some action!" Mine is this: "But things will be much more neat and tidy if we never have to mess our theories up by actually applying them." As you can imagine, we provide a useful counterbalance to each other. Nort is also a friend with whom I share certain core values—that's "values": small *v* with an *s* on the end—which can be summarized thusly: (1) in our capacity as businessmen, there is nothing more important than delivering the maximum Value to our customers; however, (2) we exist in other capacities— husband, father, son, sibling, friend, neighbor—that are more important. Striving with Nort to maintain the balance between Value and values has been an immensely gratifying struggle.

Joanna is my daughter. Mike is my son. Gail is my wife. No other words are needed to describe what they give to me and what they mean to me.

CONTENTS

Introduction 1

The Murder 5

The Investigation 23

The Solution 101

The Evidence 125

INTRODUCTION

MY NAME IS GATLING. Leonard H. Gatling. But there's no need for formalities. You can call me Gatling. Yeah, like the gun. And I've heard all the jokes, so don't waste your time trying to come up with anything new.

Anyways, I'm a cop. Which is why you coulda knocked me over with a piece of linked sausage when the publishers of this book you're holding in your hands right now, they asked me to write it. I said, "Hey, I ain't a writer! I ain't a Hemingway or any of them fancy literary types like Tom Clancy or Jackie Collins."

Or is it Joan Collins? Hell, for all I know it's *Tom* Collins. Which just goes to prove my point. Like I say, I ain't a writer. I'm a cop. That's what I do. I catch bad guys. I bust perps.

They said, "That's OK. We'll get somebody to help you with the writing."

I said, "Oh, no. Anything comes out with my name on it, I'm gonna write it."

They said, "All right. How's about we get somebody else to write this book? You help him, make sure he gets the story straight. But his name, it'll be on the cover. You just write a little piece for the beginning."

I said, "Why do you want me to write this thing so bad?" (Which is how I was afraid I would write it.)

They said, "Because you were there. You lived through this story. And it's a helluva story."

And I gotta admit. They got that part right. It is one helluva story. I been on the homicide beat now for twenty-two years—be twenty-three years in June—and I never come across anything like it. You get these business types together for one of what they call their "off-sites," you figure the biggest danger is somebody's gonna get bored to death. But you know, I found out that a lot of what goes on in them meetings is actually kinda interesting.

No, really. I mean, it ain't as exciting as—I don't know— drawing to an inside straight. But there's more going on there than you might think. Matter of fact, I discovered that I could understand a lot more about business than I thought I could. Who woulda thought that could be? An old gumshoe like me, he's able to follow what's going on in a sophisticated business meeting. And not only that, it's what helped me crack the case.

But I'm getting ahead of myself. I oughta get out of the way, let the guy they hired to write this book go to work. Guy name of Guaspari. Pretty good guy. I mean, as writers go. Let him tell you what happened. I say much more now, I'm afraid I'll spill the beans, you know what I mean?

So, there's four parts to the book you're holding in your hands right now. The Murder. The Investigation. The Solution. The Evidence. I told somebody this a coupla weeks back, and they said to me, "You shouldn't call the first part 'The Murder.' It'll spoil the suspense." I said, "You think readers are gonna be in suspense that a murder's gonna happen? It says 'murder mystery' right on the cover! What do you think they're expecting to find inside? Fondue recipes?!"

Anyways, there's four parts. And there's actually two mysteries. One is, of course, "Whodunnit?" The other one has to do with something called "the Value Effect." Lemme give you a clue: figure out what the Value Effect is, how it works, why it works . . . you got the answer to the whodunnit. At least that's how I figured it out.

And if you can't figure it out, it's all pretty much laid out for you in the part called "The Evidence." (Don't read ahead, though, 'cause that *will* spoil the suspense.) "The Evidence" ain't a story like the rest of the book is. Nobody gets whacked in that section. All the same, it's pretty interesting. Even though it's all about business. Pretty much anybody could read it and follow it. (You want proof? OK, wise guy, here's your proof: *I* could read it and follow it! Q, E, freakin', D!)

Sorry. I got a little defensive there. That's because, I gotta admit, I get thinking about all this business stuff, and I feel— What's that expression?—like a fish without water. When all this started, I wasn't really sure I wanted to have anything to do with this case. But I'm glad I did, because, like I say, it turned out to be one of the most interesting cases I've ever been on. And that's in twenty-two years in homicide, be twenty-three years in June.

Lieut. L. H. Gatling
Malibu, Kansas
December 1999

The
Murder

CHAPTER 1

For THE PAST SEVERAL YEARS, the executive team of Lodestar, Inc., had met annually for a two-day retreat at The Wayne House, one of those formerly (and formally) grand, turn-of-the-century estates that had been converted into the kind of business conference center that provides scenic vistas, the warmth of wooden appointments as opposed to standard-issue Marriott/Hyatt/Hilton brass, guests suites graced with individual and vaguely historic names, and pseudo-home-cooked meals. Of course, the meeting rooms were spectacularly unsuited to the task at hand, because matters such as sound systems, breakout rooms, and the focal length of overhead projectors tended not to be of great concern to architects who had plied their trade during the McKinley administration. But it was small and intimate, and it created the kind of atmosphere Lodestar was after.

The agenda for these annual retreats was always essentially the same: to review the status of whatever the Next Big Thing of the moment happened to be—Total Quality, Reengineering, Empowerment, Customer Focus, and the like—and to decide whether to go forward with the current Next Big Thing for another year, or to scuttle it and begin to develop the program for the *next* Next Big Thing.

So familiar was this cadence at Lodestar, in fact, that both the phrase "Next Big Thing" and its abbreviation, "NBT," had long since worked their way into the company's lexicon.

Why the seemingly constant shifting from NBT to NBT? It was a question that was often on the minds (if not the lips) of many a Lodestar employee. It was also a question for which

Lodestar President and Chief Executive Officer Bill Tollikson had a ready answer.

"We're living in a different kind of world than we came up through—or at least that some of us came up through," Tollikson would openly and earnestly explain to anyone bold enough to raise the question. "One where the only constant is change. And we can't afford to be timid or tentative about it. It's not good enough for us to merely accept change. We have to seek it out and embrace it.

"To not implement whatever seems to be emerging as the current Next Big Thing is not an option that's open to us. As a practical matter, we can either be out front with an NBT and gain the edge that it can provide. Or we can let somebody else be first and then wind up having to do it anyway, just to play catch-up.

"I prefer to lead."

In spite of the logic of their boss's position on the matter and his call for them to seek out and embrace change, though, these meetings were not something that the rest of Lodestar's executive team looked forward to. A consensus had emerged among them that these sessions, at their best, could involve some fairly stimulating discussions of some fairly interesting issues that had some fairly significant import to the company. At their worst, they became two-day gripe-fests, with blame heaped upon recrimination topped off with culpability for why yet another Next Big Thing had fallen short of its promise.

Where things normally came out was somewhere in the middle: politely tedious discussions of Next Big Thing strategies, which Tollikson's direct reports knew, in their heart of hearts, would not work—at least not as well as they had hoped they would. As a group, they may not have agreed on many things, but one thing they did agree on was this: They all believed that their time could be better spent back at the office doing *real* work rather than pretending to be enthused about admiring turn-of-the-century wall sconces and wainscoting while wearing golf shirts, drinking from coffee mugs, and doodling on note pads, all of which had been emblazoned with the logo of the NBT du jour.

Until, that is, this year. This year, the executive team was eager to attend, eager to listen, eager to learn. Why? Because they all felt that the Next Big Thing of the past year had . . . worked. By undertaking a CVC (Creating Value Connections) initiative over the past twelve months, Lodestar had achieved dramatic improvements in productivity, efficiency, market share, profitability . . . even employee morale. The mood surrounding this year's Lodestar executive retreat had a decidedly different feel to it, because the conference at The Wayne House promised to be a gratifying and uplifting two days.

In short, this year's meeting would be exciting. And this would have been true even if, over the course of those two days, there had not been three rather unusual off-agenda items:

A brutal murder.

A brilliant investigation.

The identification and incarceration of a cunning killer.

CHAPTER 2

DAY ONE of the Lodestar Executive Retreat had begun innocently enough. Michael Fallon, the lead consultant from The Condor Group, the firm that had been engaged to help guide Lodestar through the past year's Next Big Thing, was up at the front of The Wayne House's Meeting Room II (not "2" but "II": this *was,* after all, The Wayne House), busying himself with a final run-through of his checklist: overhead projector focused, extra bulb available, handouts on side table for easy access, masking tape, markers, extra easel pads, water pitcher, water glasses, reading glasses, et cetera, et cetera, et cetera. The other attendees milled around the back of the room chatting, pouring coffee, and noshing on either mixed fruit or cheese danishes, depending on just how important a role the term "heart-healthy" played in their lives.

At 7:58 a.m. Fallon's boss, Ronald Carpenter, entered Meeting Room II and headed straight for Fallon. The two had just become engaged in animated discussion—what looked to be some last-minute planning—when Fallon glanced at his watch. He was a stickler about starting on time, and 8:00 was fast approaching. Taking his cue, Carpenter made a final comment to Fallon, scribbled something on one of the flip charts Fallon had set up in front of the room, and took his seat.

Fallon checked his watch again.

"All right, all right," he intoned with mock severity. "It's time to get started. Park it anywhere."

That Michael Fallon could address the executive team of a client organization in such an irreverent fashion said a lot about the level of comfort he had with them and the degree to which he had been accepted by them. And so they did, in fact, "park it" around the three meeting tables, arranged in a U shape, with Fallon and the overhead projector stationed at the open end of the U. The seat immediately to Fallon's right remained empty, because, as the meeting's master of ceremonies and chief facilitator, Fallon had claimed it thirty minutes earlier when he had arrived to do a final check of the room's set up and some premeeting flip-charting and masking-tape tearing (two critical competencies required of any high-powered consultant).

"Good morning everyone," Fallon began. "We've got lots to cover and not a lot of time to do it in, so let's start with a quick run-through of the agenda."

He turned to the flip chart to his right and rolled its top sheet into view:

DAY 1 AGENDA

8:00-8:15	Welcome/Agenda-Review (Fallon)
8:15-8:30	~~CVC: The Bigger Picture~~ (Carpenter). *Opening Remarks*
8:30-10:00	CVC: What We Did (Bergen)
10:00-10:30	Break
10:30-11:15	Bergen (cont.)
11:15-12:15	CVC: What We Learned (Garber)
12:15-1:30	Lunch
1:30-2:30	Garber (cont.)
2:30-3:00	Break
3:00-5:00	How We Applied Those Learnings (Paulson)
5:00-6:00	Free Time
6:00-???	Dinner Meeting: NBT "Going Forward" Decision Made

"You'll notice one difference in the agenda from the one that was mailed to you. It has to do with Ronald Carpenter's remarks. Ron will have more to say about just why that change was made . . ." Fallon hesitated. For just the slightest instant it seemed as though he had something to add. Then he completed his original thought. ". . . when he gets up here in a moment."

Carol Thomas, Lodestar's vice president of Human Resources, raised her hand.

"Carol, you have a question?"

"Yes, Michael," she said. "Shouldn't we begin by sharing our thoughts about our hopes and aspirations and expectations for this meeting?"

Before Fallon could respond, Tom Magliori, the company's VP of Quality, jumped in. "But Michael's agenda has already established the requirements for the day," he said. "If we did what you're suggesting, that would introduce a variance. Would it be within tolerable limits, Michael?" Magliori smiled as he said this. He had intended his comment to be an example of the kind of "puckish Quality humor" he (incorrectly) thought he was noted for.

Fallon returned the smile. "I think you're implying that this agenda is more precise than it is," he said, responding to Magliori while artfully ignoring Thomas's suggestion.

"Hey, I got an idea," piped in John Salinsky, vice president of Sales and Marketing. "Why don't we commission a team to study the issue and share their recommendations with us before we begin?"

"Commission *this!*" offered VP of Operations Betty Bradford, laughing with Salinsky.

"All I've got to say is, the first chorus of 'Kumbaya' I hear and I'm outta here," tossed in Darren Hatfield, Lodestar's chief financial officer.

Bill Tollikson was less than pleased with the foot on which things were getting off. "I think," he said in what for him passed for stern tones, "that Michael has done a lot of work designing this meeting and that we should go with that design. Does anyone disagree?"

Silence.

"Fine," Tollikson said. "In that case, Michael, proceed."

"Sure, Bill, sure," said Fallon, pretending to search for a note on the side table in order to let the awkwardness of the moment pass. "Ah, yes. Here it is," he said, pretending to read the (blank) slip of paper he had been searching for.

"I know you all know our firm's President and Chief Executive Officer Ronald Carpenter, because he was so deeply involved in the early framing and formative stages of The Condor Group's engagement with you. In fact, such was his dedication to your success that he worked at this high level of involvement even before you decided to choose us as your consulting partner." (Hatfield, Bradford, and Salinsky—the more jaded members of the Lodestar executive team— remembered how they had felt at the time: "Sure. Bait and switch. The big guy comes in to sell the job, then they send in Skippy here to do the actual work.")

"When he heard that this meeting was being held," Fallon continued, "he asked me if he might sit in and observe. I told him that that would be OK . . . *if!* he agreed to say a few words to kick things off.

"So, Ron," Fallon said, turning to his boss and gesturing down to the point on the floor at the head of the U, "the floor is yours."

At this Carpenter slid back his chair, stood, and moved to the front of the room, giving Fallon's right shoulder a slight squeeze, just so, as they passed.

Ronald Carpenter gave off a level of gravitas that was most unusual for a man in his early forties. Ferociously bright, he was quite comfortable speaking to people in high places and quite used to being listened to by them. He cut an impressive figure, and his confident manner and bearing fueled themselves.

"Let me start by apologizing for the untidiness of the agenda," Carpenter said, as he arrived at the open end of the U and pointed to the line on the flip chart that had been crossed out—**CVC: The Bigger Picture**—and replaced with the line: **Opening Remarks.** "Don't blame Michael. Blame me." he said.

"Believe me," Salinsky said. "You really didn't have to tell us that. We already know that Mikey wouldn't be caught dead with a flip chart that looked so, so . . . so *tacky!*"

"No," Thomas added, with a smile. "Michael would never stand for such disorganization!"

Fallon's penchant for always wanting things to be "exactly right" had long since become fair game for comment. He blushed. "All right, you guys. Come on. Behave," he complained good naturedly.

Carpenter smiled, then continued. "The original plan had been for me to offer some thoughts about CVC from a broad perspective, which seemed sensible enough. When I got in last night, though, Michael and I met for a while—actually, it was early this morning. My flight got in quite late. Anyway, as we were talking, what became clear to both of us was that we had things backward. I shouldn't be talking about CVC *to* you. I should be hearing about it *from* you. My nice little ivory tower theories about 'Creating Value Connections to Effect Organizational Change' might sound nice." Carpenter's self-deprecating, mock-pompous tone drew warm smiles from his audience. "But why hear about things in theory when you can hear about how they work in the real world?

"That's what this—" he gestured toward the day's flip-charted agenda—"is all about. So, Michael and I agreed that I should make a few opening remarks and then, well, just get the hell out of the way until tomorrow morning."

More smiles, this time mixed with a few chuckles.

"Let me begin by thanking you for two things. Thank you for giving me the opportunity to be an observer at your meeting. And, even more important, thank you for your business. In the push and pull of business life, it can be easy to forget that without customers, there can be no business. So, to use the archaic but, I think, lovely phrase, 'Thank you for giving us your custom.'

"That said," Carpenter continued, "I'm here, simply, to practice what we at Condor preach. We've been working with you to help you create value connections with your customers. Well, you are our customers, and I can think of no more valuable use of my time than to connect more closely with you.

"Naturally I've been getting regular reports from Michael on what's been going on with CVC here at Lodestar. And, although these reports have been exciting and gratifying to hear, I know that it will be even more exciting and gratifying to hear more directly from the people who are actually applying it, actually engaged in it.

"I guess the only thing I have left to say is to answer a question that was posed a few moments ago." He turned to Carol Thomas and, managing a tone that was at once courtly without being condescending, said, "A fervent hope *I* have for this meeting, Ms. Thomas, is that my presence at it might in some small way add a measure of value to the proceedings."

As he said this, he bowed a charming bow in Carol Thomas's direction. Then he straightened up, smiled, and worked his way back to his seat, giving Michael Fallon another shoulder squeeze as he passed.

Fallon joined in the brief, warm applause as he reclaimed his spot at the head of the ∪. "Thank you, Ronald," he said as the applause died out, "for those observations."

"Any further changes and untidiness on the agenda are Michael's fault, not mine," Carpenter interjected, as he settled back into his chair. The room broke into laughter.

"Never happen!" Magliori said.

"Fat chance!" Bradford added.

"If you're all quite finished," Fallon said, again with a good natured smile (and, again, blushing), "are we ready to hear from some of the people who did the actual work?"

Nods all around. Fallon stepped briskly to the door of Meeting Room II, opened it, and waved in the three Lodestar associates—Sally Bergen, Ann Garber, and Peter Paulson—who had been waiting outside. As indicated on the agenda, each of the three then talked about one aspect of the CVC initiative.

Bergen focused on the specifics of what had been done: how eight, three-person teams had fanned out and engaged customers in a series of face-to-face "value conversations"; how all Lodestar functions and hierarchical levels had been represented on those teams so that the newly created value connections would go deep and wide throughout the organization; and how all twenty-four value conversation team members had come together to synthesize what they had heard into the Lodestar "value story" and offer their recommendations as to how it might be spread throughout the organization.

Garber led a discussion of the new insights the company had gained regarding what represented real value to its customers: the fact that although product price and functionality were of course important, the single biggest factor influencing Lodestar customers' buying decisions was that, "You're dependable. When you tell me you're going to do something, I know you'll do it"; the fact that the recent "improvements" to Lodestar's Web site had actually become a source of irritation to customers: "All the new bells and whistles are pretty jazzy, but I liked the old design better. It was much easier to use"; and the fact that Lodestar's business-to-business customers were looking for something much bigger than merely products and services: "What you've got to understand is that when I specify your product, I'm basically putting the relationship I have with my customer in your hands. Don't @#*% it up!" No one flinched at the vulgarity. It was what the customer had said, and Garber wanted to communicate the thought—and the emotion behind it—precisely.

Paulson presented a summary review of the actual process changes that had been (or were being) made based on the insights gained from the company's new value connections: how by taking cycle time (and therefore cost) out of the order entry process, the company could offer new, more attractive financing options to customers that would result in incremental business (and how—surprisingly enough—this idea had come from someone in Lodestar's advertising department); how by involving more customers more deeply in the new product development process, the success rate of new product introductions was trending up and the time-to-market was trending down; and how the human resources department had reengineered the company's recruiting process to ensure that only candidates likely to be compatible with the Lodestar value story would be hired (and how *this* idea had come from someone in plant management).

Compared to past NBT off-sites, the day sped by. The mood, the energy level, the degree of engagement of all participants (presenters, executive team, consultants), all day (in formal session, during breaks, over lunch), in all ways (words, actions, attitudes) were shifted virtually 180 degrees from the kind of resigned ennui that had characterized Lodestar Next Big Thing retreats in years past.

So, when Paulson completed his presentation, Michael Fallon followed by projecting an overhead transparency onto the screen:

CVC Initiative: Outcomes to Date

- Improved business results
- Achieved more quickly than had been anticipated
- With a high degree of energy and engagement to help sustain the effort going forward

At this, the Lodestar executives and Condor consultants rose and, in utter sincerity and spontaneity, gave a standing ovation to Bergen, Garber, and Paulson for the work they and their colleagues had done.

As was his way, Bill Tollikson met the three of them at the door of the meeting room and gave each a firm handshake, a warm hug, and a quiet and characteristically kind word as they departed, their work done for the day.

The three associates gone, Tollikson took up a position at the head of the U and looked at his watch. "It's five o'clock," he said.

This time it was Fallon's turn to tease.

"*Exactly* on schedule!" Fallon interjected. More laughter.

Chuckling along with the others, Tollikson asked, "We are scheduled to meet in the lobby at—when is it, Michael?"

"Six o'clock," replied Fallon.

"OK," continued Tollikson. "We're to meet in the lobby at six o'clock."

An excited cry—"*Whoop!*"—suddenly pierced the windows at the back of Meeting Room II. All heads whipped around just in time to see Bergen, Paulson, and Garber finishing off a series of high-fives, and then piling enthusiastically into Bergen's car for the short drive back to Lodestar headquarters. They were clearly exhilarated at the way their presentations had gone. Just as clearly, the Lodestar executives were exhilarated at their associates' exhilaration.

Tollikson shook his head in exaggerated puzzlement. "It's just not logical," he said.

"Don't start!" Fallon shot back.

Still more laughter.

"As I was saying before we were so delightfully interrupted by our departing associates," a beaming Tollikson continued, "we're to meet in the lobby at six o'clock sharp. We've arranged for cars to take us to a nearby restaurant for a dinner meeting at which we have a single agenda item: to decide whether we want to continue our application of CVC as next year's NBT."

The reaction—exaggerated brow-furrowing and chin scratching that said, "Gee, that's a tough one"—made it clear that the decision would be a mere formality.

Tollikson was still smiling. "Good. That should leave us plenty of time for a rather unusual activity, given the pace of things lately. It looks like we might actually be able to do some real, honest-to-goodness socializing.

"So," he said, rubbing his hands together in honest anticipation, "see you all in the lobby at six."

Tollikson stationed himself at the door to shake hands (no hugs this time: not appropriate executive-to-executive behavior) with each of his VPs and with Ronald Carpenter as they left the meeting room.

"Coming, Michael?" Tollikson asked, noticing Fallon busily working at a flip chart.

"I'll be right along, Bill. Just want to get a head start on tomorrow."

"Making sure things are exactly right, are you?"

"You got it!"

"See you at six?"

"See you at six."

* * *

Up until 6:02 p.m., the Lodestar executive retreat had gone just great. In terms of content, outcomes, logistics, esprit d'corps—on any imaginable scale, it was hard to see how things could have gone much better than they had. It was at precisely that moment that things started to go considerably less well, however, because it was at precisely 6:02 that Danny Lee, a bus boy at The Wayne House, opened the door to Meeting Room II, from which he was to clear away debris, empty water pitchers and waste baskets, and just generally set the room in order for the next day's session.

It was at precisely 6:02 and forty-five seconds that Danny Lee sprinted into the lobby of The Wayne House and shouted to the receptionist:

"Call 9-1-1! I think there's a dead guy in Meeting Room II!"

The Lodestar group, which had been milling around the lobby waiting for the restaurant carpool to form up, was paralyzed by this stun gun of a declaration. The only movement came from seven sets of eyes doing a quick visual inventory.

"Thank God," Carol Thomas said. "Everybody's accounted for."

Then Ronald Carpenter punctured the clichéd sigh of relief with a devastating question.

"Where's Michael?"

The Investigation

CHAPTER 3

"I CAME into the room and I saw him . . . just like that."

As he said this, Danny Lee pointed his thumb over his shoulder to the lifeless body of Michael Fallon, thirty feet across The Wayne House's Meeting Room II. The slightest quiver in his chin began to betray his stoicism.

"It's OK. Let it out if you have to," Homicide Detective Leonard H. Gatling reassured the boy. Gatling sat in a chair directly facing Danny Lee, no more than two feet away from him. He had been on the homicide beat for twenty-two years ("Be twenty-three years in June," he would invariably add) so he understood how unsettling and horrific a murder scene could be. For a seventeen-year-old kid to stumble into the middle of something like this . . . Well, Gatling understood that life could be pretty messy sometimes.

"Danny," he said, "I know this is hard for you, but I gotta ask you a few more questions. That OK?"

The boy nodded, his face still buried in his hands.

"OK," continued Gatling. "Now, Danny, as you were walking down the hallway to this room, did you see anyone else?"

The boy shook his head no.

"When you come into the room, did you see anything unusual?"

Danny looked up and gave Gatling a you-gotta-be-kidding-me look.

"I mean besides the body," Gatling clarified. "Did you see anything unusual besides the body?"

"I don't think so," Danny replied. "But I'm not sure. I mean, like, once I saw *that*," he gestured again with his thumb toward the body, "I didn't, like, pay a whole lot of attention to the tables or the water pitchers or that kinda stuff." Turning in his chair, he gave the room a quick once over, making sure to avoid looking at the body. "I guess it looks pretty much like these rooms always look at the end of one of these meetings."

Gatling nodded. "So lemme just review my notes, make sure I got it right. OK with you?" he said.

"OK," the boy responded, quietly.

Gatling flipped back a page or two in his notebook. "Your assignment was to come into Meeting Room II at six o'clock to clean up and get things ready for tomorrow, right?"

A nod.

"So, a coupla minutes after six, you wheeled in a cart to pick up water pitchers, glasses, plates, stuff like that, right?"

Right, Danny nodded.

"Soon as you entered the room, you see the victim. You go over to check it out, see if he's okay."

Danny buried his face in his hands and emitted a snuffling sound. Gatling took this to be an affirmative reply.

"You poke him in the shoulder, say something to him, try to wake him up. Turns out he ain't gonna answer on accounta he's dead."

Another face-buried nod.

"So, you run out to the main lobby, yell for somebody to call 9-1-1."

"Yes," croaked Danny.

Gatling scribbled some more notes on his pad.

"OK, son, that's all for now," he said, not unkindly. "You can go. But I may have to talk to you again later, got it?"

"Yes," Danny said, raising his reddened eyes. He stood up and headed for the door. Just as he reached it, he forced himself to look back at the body one more time. Then he abruptly hip-checked the brass-plated bar that spanned the width of the door and bolted from the room.

Gatling understood. He got up from his chair and walked slowly toward the body, taking care not to disturb anything or distract the forensics team from performing the ritual measuring, dusting, swabbing, recording, photographing, and other standard aspects of their ghoulishly precise craft.

He thought that he had, as the saying goes "seen it all" at more than a thousand murder scenes over his career. But this . . . *This is different,* he thought, as he looked at the deceased Michael Fallon: hands bound behind his back with CVC bumper stickers . . . gagged with a CVC T-shirt . . . multiple stab wounds inflicted by a CVC letter opener . . . battered with a blunt object—almost certainly a shattered CVC coffee mug, pieces of which were scattered here and there around the body.

In Gatling's experience, irony tended not to be at the top of most killers' priority lists, but there was no mistaking its presence here. Somebody apparently did not see the value of this CVC thing—whatever it was—and wanted to make that point abundantly clear. At this, the killer had succeeded, having slipped into Meeting Room II sometime between 5:00 and 6:00 p.m., and put this collection of CVC memorabilia to morbidly effective use.

Gatling grimaced at the thought. *Death by tchotchke.*

He allowed himself a moment to reflect on the per-verse logic of the scene. *Whoever done this done it very well,* he mused. He gave one last look at the now-late Michael

Fallon, then he wheeled and strode purposefully from Meeting Room II.

Hidden somewhere amid this horror was an elusive thing called truth. It was time for Lenny Gatling to go and find it.

CHAPTER 4

PER GATLING'S orders, The Wayne House's Meeting Room III would serve as the base camp for the investigation. He entered to find an anxiously pacing Ronald Carpenter, who, spotting Gatling, rushed across the room and peppered the detective with questions.

"What do you know? What can you tell me? How could such a thing happen? Who would do such a thing?"

Gatling held his right arm outstretched, palm out, like the traffic cop he had been twenty-some-odd years earlier. "Whoa, sport. Slow down," he said. "Let's get clear, one thing. I'm the one asks the questions. You're the one gives the answers. Got that?"

Gatling's manner with Carpenter was considerably less gentle than it had been with Danny Lee. But then Ronald Carpenter wasn't a seventeen-year-old boy, and Gatling wanted to stake out some boundaries with a man whom he had instantly sized up as someone who was used to being in charge.

Carpenter stopped, backed up a step, and held up both arms, close to his chest, palms out. A clear sign of submission.

"Of course, of course," he said, contritely. "I'm sorry. You *are* the one who asks the questions. But you have to understand that Michael was . . ." He seemed surprised and saddened at how easily he had slipped into the past tense.

Gatling lowered his arm and gestured toward a chair. Carpenter took a seat.

The detective remained standing. "Now," he said, dominance having been established, "those questions you just asked me. They were pretty good ones. So, why don't you answer them for me. What do *you* know? What can *you* tell *me?* Who *would* do such a thing?"

Carpenter shook his head slowly, forlornly.

"I haven't the foggiest," he said, still shaking his head. "I'm usually not at a loss for words, but in this case . . ." Carpenter's voice trailed off as he smiled a pained smile.

"OK," Gatling said. "I'll give you an easy question. What were you doing between five and six o'clock?"

The implication of the question drew Carpenter's eyebrows up.

"I was listening to my voice mail," he replied.

Gatling was skeptical. "For a whole hour?" he pressed.

This time Carpenter's expression was more bemused than pained.

"Yes, I'm afraid so," he answered. "When I spend all day in a meeting, I wind up with lots of messages; I had twenty-one of the damn things waiting for me when I got back to my room, a couple minutes after five."

"And you hadda answer all of 'em right then? None of 'em coulda waited?"

"Sure," Carpenter explained, "but I had to listen to all of them before I could decide which ones could wait. And that, unfortunately, takes a while."

For the time being, at least, this seemed to satisfy Gatling. "Tell me about Fallon," he said.

Hearing Michael's name spoken so matter-of-factly startled Carpenter. He paused momentarily.

"One thing I know is that Michael was—" Carpenter closed his eyes and caught himself: that past tense thing again. Regrouping, he continued. "Michael was special. We have a lot of bright, talented people at our shop. But Michael was . . . well, he was Michael is what he was."

"Yeah, fine, OK. Michael was special, Michael was Michael. I got that." Gatling was brusque. You get that way after you visit enough murder scenes. "So, tell me about this thing called CVC that was all over all the tchotchkes that done Fallon in."

"CVC was Lodestar's latest NBT," Carpenter replied.

"And how would you say that if you happened to be speaking English at the time?"

"Oh, sorry," Carpenter replied. "Like a lot of companies, Lodestar has tried a number of approaches to achieving change. Things like Total Quality, Reengineering, Empowerment, Customer Focus. Those were all big corporate efforts aimed at improving business performance. And at Lodestar they called them 'Next Big Things,' NBTs."

"What were those things all about?" Gatling asked.

"You want it in detail?" Carpenter asked.

"I'd prefer it in a nutshell."

"OK. As I understand it, Total Quality—it's sometimes called TQ—was Lodestar's first NBT. By the way, that's true for a lot of companies. A lot of organizations' first foray into large-scale change efforts happened under the Quality or Total Quality banner. Anyway, what TQ is about is eliminating defects. Reducing waste. Being more efficient. That sort of thing.

"Next came Reengineering, which said in essence: 'It's good to do things right. Better to do them fast, and lean, and right.'

"The Empowerment NBT came along to help people realize the benefits of pushing decision-making down."

"You wanna give me that again," Gatling said.

"When all decisions are made at the top of an organization, it takes too long to make things happen," Carpenter explained. "And people aren't as committed to getting the desired results because they weren't involved in the process. You empower people, you give them authority and responsibility, and those things tend to go better."

"OK," Gatling said, checking his notes. "I think there was one more . . ."

"Customer Focus. An organization that has embarked on a Customer Focus initiative is basically saying to itself: 'It's great that we're getting more efficient and involving more people in the process. It would be even better if we brought the customer's point of view into the mix.'"

"OK, fine. I got all that. So, now let's talk about their new . . . What did you call it? NBT?"

Carpenter nodded.

"Yeah," Gatling continued, "let's talk about their new NBT. CVC. The thing on the tchotchkes. That stands for what?"

"CVC stands for 'Creating Value Connections,'" Carpenter replied. "It's the term we use to describe Michael's program. . . ." Carpenter hesitated. "Well, actually it was *my* program. I invented the CVC tools and techniques Michael used with Lodestar. But that's not important. What's important is that tonight they were going to vote to continue CVC as their NBT for a second year." He paused to compose himself before adding, "That's unprecedented for a Lodestar NBT. It's a measure of what a big success CVC has been."

"Well, *you* might think that CVC was a big success," Gatling said, nodding toward Meeting Room II, "but I got a feeling there's somebody didn't think it was all that hot."

"I suppose you're right," Carpenter reflected.

"So, why don't you explain CVC to me," Gatling said.

"Details or nutshell?" Carpenter asked.

"Nutshell."

"OK," Carpenter said. "In a nutshell, CVC is all about getting an entire organization more closely and tightly connected to its customers so that it's better at understanding and then delivering what's truly of value to those customers."

Gatling scratched his head. "I know I'm no businessman," he said. "But how is that different from what you just told me was Customer Focus?"

Carpenter nodded. "A lot of people ask that question," he said. "Let me try to explain. When an organization takes on a typical Customer Focus effort, it's as if it were saying, 'We are here. The customer is over there. From time to time we will deign to look up from our work and gaze upon those customers in order to determine how what we are doing is affecting them, whether it is providing them with the optimum product/ service, and how we might need to adjust in order to better satisfy them.' And, although this is good as far as it goes, it doesn't go far enough. It's too distant. Hands off.

"CVC takes a much more aggressive posture. It gets everybody—*everybody*—into closer contact with customers. And the contact is much more active, engaging real customers in real conversation, not just reviewing survey results or observing a focus group from the other side of a one-way mirror."

"A focus what?" Gatling asked.

"Not important," Carpenter replied, shaking his head. "What *is* important are the three core assumptions CVC is based on."

"And those are?"

"For one thing, CVC assumes that what represents value for customers tomorrow will differ from what represents value for them today. That's why organizations need to be more tightly *connected to* and not just *focused on* the customer.

"It assumes that customers will not be able to directly and unambiguously articulate what those value needs of tomorrow will be. Rather, organizations will have to draw those insights by inference. To be able to do that calls for a significantly deeper knowledge and understanding of customers and their worlds, and that's another argument for closer connections with customers.

"And it assumes that opportunities for value creation lie in all corners of an organization. With everybody having direct contact with customers, mission-critical information gets directly to where it needs to be, and it gets there fast. It's not filtered through the marketing department or sales guys. Or as a client who shall remain nameless once said to me, 'With CVC, we're getting it straight from the horse's mouth, not from the other end of the horse.'"

Gatling chuckled. "That's a good one," he said.

"I thought you might like it," Carpenter said.

"So," Gatling continued, flipping back through his notes. "You're telling me that CVC was better than the other NBTs."

"Well, that's a little awkward for me to say. I mean, CVC *is* my baby," Carpenter replied.

"I'm sorry if I'm embarrassing you," Gatling said, a bit impatiently, "but I got me a murder to solve, and I ain't got time to be polite."

"OK, I understand," Carpenter nodded. "Yes, CVC is better than past NBTs. It represents the cutting edge in change strategies. The name of the game today is information flow, and CVC is all about getting the right information to the people who need it, and getting it there fast and unfiltered."

"That why CVC was gonna get a second year?" Gatling asked.

"Yes," Carpenter replied. "That and, of course, the soft stuff."

"The what?"

"The soft stuff. There's a saying I like to use, and it's that when it comes to achieving change, 'It's the soft stuff that's the hard part.' It's one thing for people to understand how to apply the hard tools and techniques of an NBT like CVC. But we're not talking about working with robots. We're talking about people. People who've got their own agendas. Who get bored. Who get distracted. Keeping people focused and enthused . . . aligned and energized. That's the soft stuff that's the hard part. The people stuff."

"Lodestar did better with the soft stuff this year?"

"If they didn't," Carpenter said, palms up, "why would they be re-upping with CVC?"

"Why did the soft stuff go better?" Gatling asked.

"Oh, I don't know," Carpenter began with an ironic expression that made it crystal clear that he did, in fact, know. "Maybe it's because for each of their past NBTs, they tried to do it themselves. They rolled their own. They gave the responsibility to one of their vice presidents and said 'run with it.' Yes, they got results for a while, but then the excitement of something being new—being next—begins to wear off. Enthusiasm wanes. People lose focus. Things begin to peter out. The NBT withers and dies.

"But this year they had a seasoned, professional consultant—Michael Fallon—guiding them through their NBT. And now they're here at the end of a year and they're still fired up. Still focused and motivated. So, what do *you* think made the difference?"

"I see your point," Gatling said.

"And you know," Carpenter said, "it's really kind of a shame. Companies spend tens of thousands of man hours—"

"Person hours."

"Excuse me?" Carpenter asked.

"I believe the preferred locution is 'person hours,'" Gatling explained. "We've had some of them consultant seminars down at the station house, you know."

"I stand corrected," Carpenter said, bowing. "They invest a ton in the tools and the techniques—the hard stuff—when what they needed all along was somebody to help with the soft stuff . . . the hard part."

"I'm beginning to get the idea that you think that the soft stuff is the hard part."

"Absolutely," Carpenter replied, oblivious to the tweak Gatling has just given him.

"So, lemme get this straight. You're saying that it's tough to get the kind of results Fallon was getting with the soft stuff?"

"Lieutenant," Carpenter said, "people would kill to get those kinds of results."

"Evidently," Gatling said.

Realizing what he had just said, Carpenter reddened. His face no longer flushed, he continued. "The hard stuff of an NBT—the specific tools and techniques that are applied—are important. NBTs come and go. But the soft stuff stays the same. It's the key. What organizations need is someone who worries about the soft stuff for them—all the time—so that people can focus on the tasks at hand . . . someone who sees it as his life's work to add to the store of knowledge about the soft stuff . . . someone who, no matter how busy he may be, is intellectually curious enough to write something like . . . something like . . ." He started to reach into his briefcase. Then he froze. "Oh, forget it. You haven't got time for this."

Gatling looked up fom his note taking. "Haven't got time for what?" he said, sharply

"This," Carpenter said. He slowly, seemingly reluctantly pulled a file folder from his briefcase. He opened it and handed its contents—a single, thick document—to Gatling.

On the upper left-hand corner of the document's first page was the logo of The Condor Consulting Group. Centered across the top of the page were the words *Interoffice Memorandum.* A few lines farther down the page, flush left, it read:

FROM: Michael Fallon
TO: Ronald Carpenter
SUBJECT: THE VALUE EFFECT
DATE: November 14, 1999

"Geez," Gatling said, feeling its heft. "This thing must be forty pages long!"

"Forty-eight," Carpenter replied.

"In case you hadn't noticed," Gatling said, gesturing toward Meeting Room II next door, "I'm a little busy right now. Why don't you just give me the highlights."

"I realize that it's a long memo," Carpenter said, apologetically. "I started to give it to you because it's the sort of thing I find really interesting, but you probably don't need to read it. Sorry."

"No, you did the right thing," Gatling assured him. "And I will take a look at it. You know, in all the spare time I got these days. For now though, why don't you give me the highlights."

"Basically, this memo discusses the ideas Michael had about something he called 'the Value Effect' and how it might explain why the soft stuff was going so well at Lodestar. You can see from the date—yesterday—that even though he was up to his eyeballs preparing for the Lodestar meeting, Michael was working on this memo. So, he was obviously quite excited about it. He left a copy for me Sunday night because he thought some of the ideas in it might be useful in my presentation on Monday morning."

Gatling interrupted. "The one that was crossed out on the agenda in the other room over there? That the one you're talking about?"

"Exactly," Carpenter replied. "Well, as much as I wanted to get to bed Sunday night—it was *very* late when I got in—I figured that I owed it to Michael to at least read his memo. I did, and I liked it a lot. In fact, I got so excited I went straight to his room. I knew he'd still be up. I said, 'This is great! I can't wait to share it with Lodestar tomorrow!' By the time I got there, though, he had gotten cold feet. He was worried that he hadn't thought things through well enough to go public with the Value Effect just yet. Michael always wanted to do things exactly right, which is good, but sometimes it can be a problem. It can paralyze you. I thought that the ideas were solid and that they could add a lot to my presentation. We discussed it for a while, for quite a while, actually. It was about three in the morning when we agreed to a compromise. I'd get to talk about the Value

Effect, but I'd have to wait until Tuesday. That would give Michael more time to think things through. You know, to make sure things were exactly right. I hated to wait, because this was all about the soft stuff, and it's the soft stuff . . ."

". . . that's the hard part. Believe me, I got it." Gatling made little attempt to hide his exasperation.

"Sorry," Carpenter said, abashed.

Gatling looked once more at the memo before adding it to the pile of papers on the table next to him. "I'll look at it when I get a few minutes where I can take a breath. When that'll be, who knows?"

"Might help, might not," Carpenter said, with a shrug. "I guess you ought to be the judge of that, shouldn't you?"

"Yeah, I should," Gatling said, shifting gears. "You got any idea who might have made Fallon turn toes up?"

"Michael didn't have an enemy in the world," Carpenter said, blanching at Gatling's horrifyingly blasé phrasing of the question.

Gatling cocked his head. "Seems to me he had at least one, don't ya think?"

Carpenter shrugged.

"Who do you suppose it could be?" Another shrug. Gatling was unconvinced. "I think you got some suspicions who mighta done this but don't wanna say."

"Well," Carpenter began, with something of a resigned grimace, "if you look at it one way, there were several people who might have had a reason to do this."

"Name me one."

"I really don't think it's appropriate for me to say."

"Appropriate is nice. But I got me a dead body next door that trumps appropriate. So like I say, name me one."

"Well," said Carpenter, straining, fighting with himself. "It actually could have been any of them."

"Any of who?"

"Any of the executives who were in that meeting today," he nodded toward Meeting Room II next door, "could have done it."

"Why?"

"Because almost every executive in that meeting room was responsible for an initiative that had fallen short in the past. Magliori ran the Total Quality program. Salinsky was in charge of Customer Focus. Carol Thomas was in charge of Empowerment. Bradford had Reengineering. Because he was the big boss, Tollikson in effect ran them all. And because he's the CFO, Hatfield paid for them all. Now Michael comes along and succeeds where all of them failed, and that makes them all look bad. And people don't like to look bad. Especially people with big titles and egos to match."

Gatling was intrigued. "Let me ask you something," he said. "I know more than I'd like to know about all this murder stuff. It's my business. When it comes to some of the stuff you were talking about, like Total Reengineering and Empowered Quality and NBTs and CVSs and all the rest, though, I can't say I know much about those kinds of things. So, I'm thinking, maybe you can help me understand the business side of all this. You know, behind the scenes, help me sort through what I'm gonna hear when I talk to the others."

Carpenter brightened. "What you want is for me to be your shadow consultant!"

"Wha . . . ?"

"Shadow consultant. It's a term we use," Carpenter explained. "Never mind. The answer is yes, of course. I will do anything I can to help."

"Yeah, thanks," Gatling said. "And stay close by. I'll call you when I need you."

"You got it," Carpenter said. "I owe it to Michael. Or at least to his memory. In fact, you want to get a good feel for just how good Michael Fallon was at what he did? Ask all of the Lodestar folks about the soft stuff that we've been talking about. Ask them what Michael Fallon was doing to make the soft stuff go better. They won't be able to tell you, and that's because Michael was so skillful at it. His contribution didn't show. He kept the spotlight on them.

"And the thing he called the Value Effect—most guys, if they came up with something that good, they'd be shouting it from the rooftops. Not Michael. In fact, I'll bet that if you asked the Lodestar executives whether Michael had ever mentioned the Value Effect to them, they'd all say no. In fact, I guarantee it. Michael would say, 'It's my job to worry about that stuff so they can stay focused on their work. That's the value *I* add.'

"Like I told you a few minutes ago, Michael didn't want to talk about the Value Effect at all at this meeting. I had to insist. Even then, it had to wait until Tuesday so that he could get it exactly right. And now . . ."

Carpenter let the thought trail off as he sadly got up and walked to the door of Meeting Room III. As he reached it, he stopped and turned back to face Gatling.

"Lieutenant?"

"Yeah?"

"You said that the questions I asked you when you first came into this room were pretty good ones. 'What do you know?' 'What can you tell me?' 'Who would do such a thing?'"

"Yeah, so. What about 'em?"

"You left one out," Carpenter said.

"Which one?"

"The one about 'How *could* such a thing happen?'"

"I didn't ask it because I already know the answer."

"You do?"

"Yeah, I do."

"What's the answer? How could such a thing happen?"

"Such a thing could happen on accounta it happened."

"I don't follow."

"When you've been at this sort of thing as long as I have, you realize there's no point in asking 'How could it happen?' These things happen 'cause they happen. Life is complicated. There's no easy answers. It's just the way it is, that's all. Spend too much time asking 'How could such a thing happen?' you make yourself crazy."

"Oh." And with that, Carpenter lowered his eyes and exited Meeting Room III.

Gatling followed him out to the door a moment later and called to the uniformed officer standing guard outside Meeting Room II. "Bring me the Quality guy, Magliori."

Then he went back into Meeting Room III and waited patiently. All those years in homicide had taught him a lot. One thing they had taught him was that the truth could not be rushed. It would make itself known, at its own pace and in its own way. In the meantime, it was his job to be there—steady, resolute—when it happened.

It was the least he could do for this guy Fallon, thought twenty-two-year veteran homicide detective Leonard H. Gatling. Be twenty-three years in June.

CHAPTER 5

THE DOOR to Meeting Room III cracked open several inches. When no one squeezed through, Gatling leaned back in his chair to give himself a clearer line of sight through the crack, out into the hallway. All he could see was the partial silhouette of a smallish man. The reflection from a Wayne House hallway lamp shone off the man's eyeglasses like the running lights on a late-model car.

"When the officer told you to come in," Gatling called to the silhouette, "he meant *all the way* in, ya know?"

The door opened a bit wider, and Tom Magliori—dubbed "the Human Pocket Protector" by Betty Bradford—edged into Meeting Room III. Gatling motioned to the seat that had just been occupied by Ronald Carpenter. Magliori quickly took it, compliance being a value held dearly by VPs of Quality.

And when it came to Total Quality (TQ, in the industry lexicon), Magliori was, to put it mildly, a true believer in all that it represented. When, years earlier, he had attended his first TQ seminar and heard that "quality is a way of life," his only objection had been that such a pronouncement didn't go nearly far enough. In the too-brief life span of the company's formal Total Quality program, however, he had managed to take what is arguably the most powerful set of tools and principles that a business organization has at its disposal to achieve what's come to be called "world-class" performance and turn virtually the entire workforce against them.

Tedious and *dull* were the words that some people used when the topic on the table was TQ. And these were Magliori's allies. The vast majority of the organization had a somewhat edgier viewpoint on the topic, peppering their language with words such as *bureaucratic, threatening,* and *insulting.*

Magliori's response when confronted by Bill Tollikson with this information? "Let's do some fishboning so that we can get to the root cause of the problem!" Shortly thereafter, Total Quality as a formal Lodestar program died. Few mourned its passing. Magliori stayed on in a more traditional quality role: more technician, less Svengali.

Now he looked up expectantly, waiting for Gatling to speak first.

"I'm Lieutenant Gatling. I'll be heading up this investigation. I need to ask you a few questions."

"I'll answer as best I can," Magliori said, helpfully.

"Good. So tell me, where were you between five and six o'clock this evening?"

Magliori stiffened. "Are you suggesting that I'm a *suspect?*"

"In my world," Gatling shrugged, "there's two kindsa people—dead ones and suspects. At least that's how it is at the beginning of a case. I do my job right. I start crossing names off the list of suspects. When there's just one name left, I'm done. So, don't take it personal."

Though a bit unsettled by Gatling's gruff frankness, Magliori, ever the professional, appreciated the logic and discipline of the detective's approach.

"OK," Magliori said, a bit sheepishly, "I'll try not to."

"Good," Gatling said. "So, like I was saying, where were you between five and six o'clock tonight?"

"My goodness," Magliori faltered, still off balance from the unexpected line of inquiry. "Given the horrible thing that's happened, it's kind of hard to be very precise about that."

"Do your best."

"OK. Well, let's see." Magliori searched his memory. "The meeting adjourned at five-oh-two. I went straight to my room. Got there at, what, five-oh-three? five-oh-four? I called in to pick up my voice mail messages. There were eleven of them. By the time I listened to and responded to all of those, it was five forty-four or so. Then I called my wife and kids to say hello. At five-fifty-eight, I went down to the lobby. We were supposed to meet there at six o'clock to go out to dinner. But then, well, you know. All of *this* happened." And as he said "this," Magliori waved both hands in the air, pivoting at the wrists like twin propeller blades.

"Makes sense to me," Gatling scribbled in his notebook. "So, tell me about Fallon. What kinda guy was he?"

Magliori smiled sadly. "I don't use words like this lightly," he began, "but I can say without any hesitation that Michael Fallon was a six-sigma performer."

"Six *what*-ma?"

"Six 'sigma,'" Magliori explained. "It's a quality expression. It means that, for one thing, Michael was utterly reliable. When he said he was going to do something, he did it. He did it right, and he did it on time, and he did it well."

"So, in your book, that's what it takes to be six whatchamacallit?"

"It's part of it, but it's not the whole story," Magliori continued. "Michael also was world class at being data driven."

"Data driven? What'sat?"

"He didn't make decisions or judgments based on opinion or gut feel. His recommendations were based on numbers, metrics. You know, *real* stuff governed by the laws of statistics and physics, not wish lists and pet peeves. That's one of the things that makes CVC—Michael's NBT—so good. Because people are talking directly to customers, the signal-to-noise ratio is high."

Gatling's instincts told him to move on without asking.

"Anything else?"

"He understood and respected process."

"Why's that so important?"

"Because when you're trying to do things right the first time—and do them right reliably and repeatably—then the proper unit of analysis is the work process, not the department or the person or the task or whatever other red herring people tend to get distracted by."

"If you say so," Gatling said, scribbling notes. "Anything else?"

"Well, there wasn't an arrogant bone in his body."

"That's unusual?"

"Unusual?" Magliori said, eyes widening, eyebrows arching. "Why, nonarrogant consultants are practically unheard of. On the bell curve of consultant arrogance, Michael was out there to the left, a good eight-, maybe even *ten*-sigma!"

"I thought sigma was six?"

"No, you see, sigma is—never mind. Let's just say that, yes, it is very unusual for a consultant not to be arrogant. Usually what happens is they come in as if they have *the* answer—God's gift to management. But Michael didn't do that"

"He ever say anything to you about something called 'the Value Effect'?"

"No. Should he have?" Magliori asked, anxiously.

"No, not really. Just something I heard about," Gatling said, scribbling his notes (and leaving Magliori more anxious than ever). Gatling flipped back several pages in his notepad, then took his line of questioning in a slightly different direction. "Lemme see . . . if I got it right, you were responsible at one time for the company's 'Total Quality Program'?"

Magliori stiffened. "No, that is *not* right."

"Geez, I musta got something wrong then," Gatling said, puzzled, again consulting his notes, "'cause I thought that's what your job was here."

"My job has never been to run a Total Quality 'program,'" Magliori replied, regaining a bit of his composure. "TQ is not a 'program.' TQ is a set of principles, a management philosophy . . . a way of life."

"Sorry. I stand corrected," Gatling said. "But you *are* responsible for what you called TQ, right?"

"That's right," Magliori replied, somewhat mollified.

"And at one point, TQ was a—whattayacallit?—an 'NBT'?"

"It was."

"So, your current NBT, CVC. It was compatible with TQ?" Gatling was becoming quite facile with abbreviations.

"Oh my, yes, fully compatible!" Magliori intoned without a second's hesitation. "CVC applies many of the same principles as TQ. It's helped us to achieve some of the TQ goals we've been after for years."

"What about the soft stuff? The people stuff? Was that going any better with CVC than it did with your NBT?"

"Well, CVC did seem to get people more aligned and energized. Michael used those terms—'aligned' and 'energized'—all the time. Almost like a mantra."

"So, what was it that Fallon did to get people aligned and energized?

"Let's see . . . for one thing—" Magliori stopped suddenly. What had started as an energetic response to Gatling's seemingly simple question had fizzled. He was surprised that he had to grope for an answer.

"I'm waiting," Gatling said, phlegmatically.

Magliori continued to grope.

"One of the things that, uh, that Michael would do would be to, uh . . . whenever there was a, uh, situation . . ."

Gatling said nothing. He merely arched his eyebrows and held his pen poised, expectantly, over his notebook.

"Because Michael was, well, Michael," Magliori finally said, frustrated at his inability to come up with anything more specific.

This seemed to exasperate Gatling. "Why does everybody keep telling me, 'Michael was Michael'? Do you think I have a hard time accepting that Michael was Michael? Understanding that Michael was Michael? I mean, it's a *tautology*, for cryin' out loud!" He paused. Cooling off, he mercifully let Magliori off the hook. "OK. That's all I need from you for now. Don't go too far. I may need to talk to you again."

"I'm not going anywhere," Magliori said, "except back to my room. Call me if you need me."

Then he rose and walked, dejectedly, from The Wayne House's Meeting Room III.

* * *

"He said *what?!*" an incredulous Ronald Carpenter asked, barely having sat down in The Wayne House's Meeting Room III for his first shadow consultation with Lenny Gatling.

"He said that . . . lemme see here . . ." Gatling searched through his notes until he found the entry he was looking for. "Yeah, here it is. He said that CVC was, quote, 'fully compatible' with TQ. And you ain't buying that?"

"Not *buying* that?!" Carpenter was more incredulous than ever. "Saying that CVC is fully compatible with TQ is like saying that the engine in my Mercedes is fully compatible with the cigarette lighter. Strictly speaking, I suppose it's true, but we've got some serious apples and oranges problems at work here."

"Why's that?"

"Look. TQ—Total Quality, or Total Quality Management, or whatever you want to call it—was the Next Big Thing ten, maybe fifteen years ago, but it never lived up to its promise. It was oversold."

"Magliori said that it was . . ." Gatling rifled again through his notepad. "'A way of life.'"

"Bingo! What did I tell you? Guys like Magliori make it sound like TQ is the way and the truth and the light, but it isn't. Don't get me wrong. It can be very effective. TQ is a set of tools and techniques and principles that can be very powerful in helping organizations improve performance, but 'a way of life' it isn't."

"Then why'd he say it is?" Gatling asked.

"Because he really believes that it is," Carpenter replied. "That's how he got to be a big shot at Lodestar. He rode the TQ movement to an executive position. Before TQ, the Quality department was a corporate ghetto. All of a sudden, he's a star, and that's pretty heady stuff. Then TQ crashes and burns, and he's not such a big star anymore."

"Why'd it crash and burn?"

"First, like I said, it was oversold. More than that, though, TQ bores the hell out of people. Applying the principles of TQ means a lot of planning and detail and standards and specifications. All the stuff that makes people crazy. You can put all the nice words on it that you want to, but at the end of the day, it feels bureaucratic as hell. And it's insulting to people, too."

"How so?"

"Think about it. You've worked hard at your job and one day management announces that we're going to start a new Quality program."

"Magliori said it wasn't a program."

"He might have said it wasn't a program, but when you rent a hotel ballroom, hold an all-hands meeting, print posters and bumper stickers, have an open bar, and give everybody cheese and crackers and Swedish meatballs, what you've got is a program, my friend."

"I s'pose."

"Anyway, you work hard, and one day management announces the new Quality program, and you wind up asking yourself, 'Don't they think I've been doing a quality job up until now?' When that happens, I don't care how good the Swedish meatballs are, you feel insulted."

"He also said that CVC helped the company reach a lotta the TQ goals he was after, though, and that he didn't care if they called it something else or if somebody else got the credit."

"I can buy the first part of that, but not the second," Carpenter said. "Damn right CVC helped them achieve their TQ goals. If he's anything like the other TQ types I've met, though, Magliori is viewed by people as a bureaucrat. You know, a cop."

"And the problem with that is . . . ?"

"Oh, yeah," Carpenter chuckled, slightly flustered. "Sorry about that. Michael came in and got those results without boring people, without insulting people, without claiming to be the way and the truth and the light. He did it in a way that respected and energized them. I'm not buying this 'who cares if we called it something else so long as we got the results' bushwa. Any way you slice it, he made Magliori look bad."

"There's one other thing that was interesting," Gatling said, looking down at his notes. "He had good things to say about Fallon as a man. Called him, lemme see . . . where did that go? Called him 'reliable' . . . 'data driven' . . . some six thing or other."

"Six sigma," Carpenter offered.

"Yeah, that's it. Six what you just said."

"Doesn't surprise me."

"No, but when I asked him what Fallon did to make the CVC thing work so well, he couldn't come up with anything. Made it sound like Fallon was a good guy and all, but he didn't exactly *do* much of anything to make CVC go."

"Oh, for godsakes!" Carpenter said, throwing up his hands. "That's exactly the point I was trying to make when we talked earlier. Magliori can't figure out why CVC was working so well. But they had a pro helping them. Keeping them focused and aligned. Dealing with the soft stuff. Somebody who's up until two o'clock on the night before an important client meeting thinking about things like the Value Effect."

"He said he'd never heard of the Value Effect," Gatling said.

"That doesn't surprise me. Or bother me. That's our job, not his. What does get my goat is when people don't give us our due . . . or, I should say, give Michael *his* due. I mean, the man gave his life to these people. Literally gave his *life!*" Carpenter took a moment to cool down. "Then again, that's exactly what made Michael so good. So, if Magliori couldn't see what Michael was doing, that means Michael was doing it skillfully, adroitly. But I have my doubts."

"Doubts about what?"

"About whether Magliori really couldn't see what it was that Michael was doing."

"How do you mean?" Gatling asked.

"Think about it," Carpenter said, eyes flashing. "My guy comes in, makes it look easy. That makes Magliori look even worse. So he puts him down, as if Michael was just there to serve coffee and be charming. Believe me, he knows that Michael brought a *lot* to the party—a lot more than Magliori brought."

"Hmm," said Gatling, noncommittally. Then he scanned his notes one more time. "One of the last things he said was, 'I don't think we'll get the same kinds of results without Michael.'"

"Now *that*," Carpenter replied, pointing a finger at Gatling's notepad for emphasis, "is one thing that he got right."

"Maybe not just right," added Gatling. "Maybe dead right."

CHAPTER 6

Betty BRADFORD was the next name on Lenny Gatling's list. As VP of Operations, she was unabashedly interested only in what she called "The three Ps: Phriggin' Productivity and Profitability." Bradford actually had seen some benefit from two of the Next Big Things that had been tried at Lodestar. She had initially liked the rational, data-driven rigor that went with TQ, but her interest waned when she sensed how slow and bureaucratic it all had begun to feel. ("ISO schmiso! I want results, not certifications!" she once declared during a memorable address to a group of securities analysts.) She had also enthusiastically embraced Reengineering, actually honchoing the company's Reengineering program until Bill Tollikson came to realize that all the efficiency and productivity gains were being made at the expense of the company's heart and soul. (To this day, Bradford remained uncontrite. "Several million bucks for a few fewer hugs. Still seems like a damn good trade-off to me," was the bottom line summary she was utterly uninhibited about voicing.)

The late evening light refracted through The Wayne House's century-old window glass gave her entrance a dramatic cast as she stalked through Meeting Room III and plunked herself down in a chair without waiting for an invitation from Gatling to do so. Stalking and plunking came naturally to Bradford. This damn-the-torpedoes approach combined with her not inconsiderable girth to imbue Bradford with an almost palpable kinetic sense, and her opening question to Gatling did nothing to slow that momentum down.

"So what can I do you for, Kojak?"

"The name is Gatling," he said. The edge in his voice was unmistakable.

"Yeah, sure, Gatling. I know," Bradford replied. "I was just trying to lighten things up is all. I mean, there's some pretty heavy stuff goin' on around here. Sorry."

Gatling let it pass. "Where were you between five and six o'clock this evening?" he asked.

Bradford burst out laughing. "I'm sorry, I'm sorry." She held up her hands and shook her head. "But I mean, 'Where were you between five and six o'clock?' You really *ask* that question? Isn't that kind of a cliché? I feel like I'm watching a phriggin' movie!"

This time Gatling didn't let it pass. "You think you're watchin' a phriggin' movie, do ya? Then why don't you ask Fallon in there—" He jerked his head in the direction of Meeting Room II. "—to buy you some phriggin' popcorn!"

"You're absolutely right," Bradford said, managing to wipe almost all of the smile from her face. "I was way outta line. I'm sorry."

"OK," Gatling said. "Let's try it again. Where were you between five and six o'clock tonight?"

"I went into the bar for a quick pop," she replied. "Ask the bartender. His name's Ted."

"Didn't you have to check your messages? There's a break, ain't that what you management types do?"

"Did it on this," she said, pulling a cellular phone from the pocket of her blazer. "When I saw our people starting to congregate in the lobby—the bar is right off the lobby—I settled up with Ted and that was that."

Satisfied by the answer, although still put off by her tone, Gatling pressed on.

"Tell me about Fallon."

"How do you mean?" Bradford asked

"However you want it to mean," Gatling came back.

"Pretty good guy. Good at what he did."

"I keep hearing people say how 'reliable' he was," Gatling said. "That sound right to you?"

"*Reliable!?*" Bradford laughed. "How about: 'You-couldn't-pull-a-pin-out-of-his-butt-with-a-tractor!' He was—How shall I say?—just a touch too worried about the details."

Gatling sensed a bit of rancor. "You have a problem with Fallon?" he asked.

"No," Bradford replied. "I got along pretty good with him. But I have to admit that I do have a problem with consultants in general."

"Why's that?"

"Because they forget that we're here to run a business, not to be a playground for a bunch of wet-behind-the-ears MBAs who've got a lot of dollars but no sense, if you get my drift." She pulled a pack of cigarettes from her purse. "OK with you?" she asked.

"Smoke 'em if you got 'em," he shrugged. She lit up.

"What consultants forget," she said, pausing for a deep drag on her cigarette, "is that what they do is inherently an imposition. I mean, *they're* the ones who call it 'an intervention.'"

"Fallon was like that?"

"Not too bad, as consultants go. Better than some, I guess. At least the CVC stuff he did was down to earth, pretty straightforward. Not a lot of consultant b.s. I mean, we worked with him for what, about a year? And not once in that entire time did he draw a 2 × 2 matrix. I think consultants are required to reduce everything to a 2 × 2 matrix, but he never did. I used to tell him that if that ever got out, he probably would have been drummed out of the corps. He'd laugh and say, 'You're prob'ly right.'"

"What else was good about this CVC thing?"

Bradford sat forward and released parallel streams of smoke through her nostrils, "It said, straight up, 'The reason value is important is that it's what makes customers buy. So, you want to do the things that make customers buy and stop doing the things that don't.'"

"Sounds obvious," Gatling said, a bit skeptical.

"It *is* obvious, but most consultants aren't interested in what's obvi-*ous*. Most consultants obfus-*cate*. In general, Michael didn't do that." She gave Gatling a triumphal smile. "Bet you didn't think I knew words like that, did ya?" she barked with a smoky chortle.

Gatling couldn't help himself. A small smile of his own leaked out as he continued to scribble in his notebook.

"So, this CVC thing," he said. "Net. A good thing? A bad thing?"

"Oh," she said, taking one final drag before stubbing the cigarette out on the rim of the empty soft drink can she carried with her for precisely this use, "as NBTs go, a good thing, I guess."

"Why?"

"Because it supports what I think should be the first commandment of any business."

"And what's that?"

"When they make me queen, this is what I'm gonna have chiseled on everybody's forehead: 'The customer has the money, and we want it.' Everybody keeps that in mind, you're gonna do better. And CVC is all about that. Maybe Fallon prettied it up a bit. He was always talking about getting everybody 'aligned and energized.' And there was that business about 'customer-ness' he'd lay on us every once in a while, but I could live with that because it kept us focused on what made customers give us their money. Call me a cockeyed optimist, but I like it when customers give us their money. I think that's a good thing."

"You were in charge of one of Lodestar's other Next Big Things, weren't you?" Gatling asked.

"Oh, yeah," Bradford replied with just the slightest rolling of her eyes. "I was the tsar—I guess it would be tsarina—of Reengineering."

"And it didn't work?"

"Oh, it worked fine. We got some good results."

"Work as well as CVC?"

"On the hard stuff, pretty much. I mean, there's a lot of similarity."

"I'm not following."

"Look, you talk about Reengineering, you're gonna be talking about value until it's comin' outta your ears," Bradford explained. "The whole point of Reengineering is to map out a process, determine which steps add value and which ones don't, and keep doing the ones that do and stop doing the ones that don't. Value-added is what it's all about. CVC is just another way of getting at those same principles."

"So, you saw what Fallon was doing as supporting what you had tried to do?"

"Absolutely."

"By the way," Gatling asked, as though distracted by something he had seen in his notebook. "You said something about value 'comin' outta your ears.' Did Fallon ever mention anything to you about something called 'the Value Effect'?"

"Not that I can remember," she said.

"No sweat," Gatling replied, innocently. "It came up in another conversation, and I wondered if it had with you."

"Nope."

"Back to CVC. Why do you think it worked better than Reengineering?"

"Well," Bradford said with a rueful smile. "In case you hadn't noticed, I can be a little rough around the edges. I don't have the patience to spend a lot of time making nice-nice with people so they'll decide to buy into the program."

"And Fallon did?"

"I don't know. I guess he was better at the soft stuff. And if that's what it would take to make things work—to get customers to give us their money—well then, God bless Michael."

Bradford stopped for a moment, reflecting on what she had just said. Then she said it again, in a tone that wasn't rough around the edges at all. "God bless Michael."

Gatling somberly nodded. The interrogation was over. "Don't go too far," he said, as Bradford got up to leave.

"Oh, don't worry, Koj—er, Gatling. I won't."

It was getting late. Gatling was tired. He decided to let it pass again.

* * *

"Betty Bradford used the term 'nice-nice'?" Ronald Carpenter asked. "I mean, I know I haven't spent that much time with her, but I find that hard to believe."

"Well, she said it," Gatling replied. "She said that the reason her Reengineering program didn't work as well as CVC worked as an NBT is that she didn't have time to make nice-nice so that people would decide to buy in to the program but that it kinda came natural to Fallon."

"She thought that was all that Michael did? That he made nice-nice?"

"She said he did more. Had a hard time comin' up with any specifics, though."

"What did I tell you?" he said, punctuated by a skeptical snort. Then he shook his head in disgust. "She doesn't have a clue about what Michael was doing. I'll bet she didn't know anything about the Value Effect, either, did she?"

Gatling shook his head.

"Figures. Anyway, I have another real problem with what she said."

"What's that?"

"It's this whole business about people 'deciding' not to buy into a Reengineering program. People 'decide' not to buy into Reengineering in the same way—and for approximately the same reason—that people hiding in closets from ax murderers 'decide' not to hum. There are some things that you just sort of *know*."

Gatling shook his head. "You're losin' me."

"Look. Bradford was right when she said that the idea of value-added is at the heart of Reengineering. When you do Reengineering work, you *do* map out work processes, and you *do* identify the steps that add value and the steps that don't, then you *do* stop doing the steps that don't and keep doing the steps that do."

"Yeah," Gatling said. "That's pretty much what Bradford said."

"Sure," Carpenter said. "Think about what it implies when you stop doing the things that don't add value. What do you suppose happens then?"

Gatling shook his head, still perplexed.

Carpenter prompted him. "Fewer steps in the process means . . ."

The light went on for Gatling. "Fewer jobs for people?" he said.

"Bingo. The trouble is that being asked to be part of a Reengineering team . . . by the way, isn't it great that all you have to do these days is call something a 'team' and all of a sudden it *must* be a good thing? Anyway, being asked to be part of a Reengineering team is like being asked to go on a suicide mission. The techniques work, but after you apply them, fewer people *have* work. Betty Bradford can give you her brassy, bottom-line routine and say that what Michael was doing was supportive of what she had been doing all along. But here's the real bottom-line: She ran the Reengineering program and it failed as an NBT. Then Michael came in and showed people that you can make change happen that will cause customers to give you their money without having to slash and burn the organization in the process. He made Betty Bradford look bad. And it's my guess that she doesn't like to be made to look bad."

"Well," Gatling said, with a world-weary sigh, "maybe she looked bad when her Next Big Thing failed, but you know what?"

"What?" replied Carpenter.

"She doesn't look half as bad as Michael Fallon looks right about now."

CHAPTER 7

*N*ICE WAS THE WORD most often used to describe Carol Thomas, the company's VP of HR, and people didn't always—or even generally—mean it as a compliment. It wasn't that she didn't care about business success (a sign posted on a wall in her office read: "Healthy Finances Lead to a Healthful Workplace!"), it was just that it was not deeply embedded in her bones in the way that her concern for "her people" was. A content analysis of all her written and spoken communications of the past year would undoubtedly have revealed that the words most commonly used by her had been *share, open-door,* and *empower.* In fact, she had run Lodestar's Empowerment program until the fateful day when Bill Tollikson walked into her office, closed the door, and shared with her the news that the Empowerment program was at an end. Her response had been to spend a sleepless night fretting about the angst it surely must have caused Tollikson to have had to share what he surely must have perceived as such distressing news.

Her initial words upon entering The Wayne House's Meeting Room III were perfectly in character. "This must be very difficult for you," Thomas said as she settled into the chair that Lenny Gatling had proffered her.

"Not nearly as difficult as it is for Fallon," Gatling said.

"No, I don't suppose it is," Thomas said, her already reddened eyes welling up again. She was quite short and quite slight, and her tearfulness made her appear almost painfully frail. Yet she leaned forward, ever solicitous. "But what must your job be like, dealing with this kind of grief and horror, hour after hour, day after day. Trafficking almost exclusively within the darkmost corners of human nature. Performing a sort of septic system maintenance service for society, examining the detritus of the human spirit as it leeches out and infects the lives of others. How *do* you do it?"

"It's a living," Gatling said in the off-hand way you say such things after twenty-two years on the homicide beat. "Look, I've gotta ask you some questions that are kinda difficult."

"And in asking them," Thomas offered, "you are truly doing God's work."

"Yeah, well, whatever," Gatling said. "Anyway, where were you between five and six o'clock tonight?"

She winced before answering the question and dabbed at her eyes with an already saturated handkerchief.

"After we adjourned our meeting at five o'clock, I went back to my room to drop off my things—portfolio, handouts from the meeting, message slips: those sorts of things. I called in to check for my voice mail messages. Then I went down to the lobby at five-thirty to meet with Bill Tollikson. He wanted to share some of his thinking about a new benefits program we're going to introduce to our associates next month. The others started arriving in the lobby at about five or ten before six, so that cut our discussion a bit short. That's when that boy came into the lobby—"

She put her hand to her mouth and was reasonably successful at holding back her emotions, with only the odd sob or two escaping.

Gatling grimaced his support, but duty compelled him to move on.

"How would you describe Fallon?"

"Dependable as the day is long," she said, her face brightening for the first time. "Always talked about trying to do things exactly right, and that's usually how he did them. He was truly a helper. Truly facilitative in his ability to help us stretch out to reach our full potential."

"Any way you can be a little more specific than that?"

"What do you mean?"

"I dunno. I guess, *how* he helped you is what I'm lookin' for."

"I told you," she answered. "He was facilitative."

"That's it?"

"What else is there?"

"I see," Gatling lied. "Anyway . . . this CVC thing he was helping you with. Was it a good thing? You support it?"

"Oh my goodness, yes," Thomas said, with the look on her face registering disbelief that the question even had to be asked.

"Why's that?"

"Because it truly *involves* our people. It comes from a place that truly respects them and the contribution they make to the corporate enterprise. It involves all corners of the organization. It aligns people. In today's meeting we heard from three people who headed up CVC project teams. They were energized because based on the work done by those teams, we—the management team of the company—have been making decisions and taking action. That is Empowerment—*real* Empowerment—at its most powerful."

"Powerful Empowerment?" replied Gatling.

"Yes, you might put it that way," said Thomas, not catching the touch of sarcasm in Gatling's tone.

"Fallon ever say anything to you about something called the Value Effect?"

"No," Thomas replied. "But it certainly sounds intriguing."

"Yeah, well, whatever," Gatling said, waving the matter away. "What were we talking about?"

"Empowerment, I think," Thomas said.

"Right. Empowerment. Didn't you have some kinda formal Empowerment program at Lodestar a while back? Weren't you the person who headed it up?"

"Yes, we did. And yes, that NBT was mine."

"Would you say it was successful?"

"I think so. Our Empowerment efforts did a lot, I think, to sensitize people to the holistic nature of the enterprise. It gave them a set of lenses through which they could see how their efforts affected what Lodestar as an entire organization could accomplish. It helped to validate people's contributions and make them feel better about themselves. So, yes, I'd call it a success."

Gatling strove mightily to keep his bearings amid this onslaught of HR-speak. Of course, being a homicide detective, he didn't know that it *was* HR-speak. What he did know was that it was not the sort of language you tended to hear around murder scenes.

"Would you say that what Fallon was doing supported what you were trying to do?"

"Yes, exactly!" Thomas replied, excitedly. "You've put your finger on it! In effect, what you're saying is that CVC is the vessel that gave shape and meaning to Empowerment as it was poured into the organization!"

"I am?" Gatling asked, puzzled.

"Oh, yes, absolutely!" Thomas enthused.

"If you say so," he said.

Thomas's delight was short-lived, however, as it dawned on her that, as she then so morosely put it, "Michael's departure from this mortal coil will have the effect of causing a crack in the vessel of our Empowerment."

Even as hard-boiled a detective as Gatling was he couldn't help but be affected by her utter ingenuousness. "Thank you for, uh, sharing," he said, with the last word sounding as though it had been pulled from him with a pipe wrench, "your thoughts and impressions at what I know is a difficult time. Please stay close by. 'Cause I may need to question you some more."

"I'll be happy to," Thomas said. Then, realizing the incongruity of that happiness, she covered her mouth yet again, sobbed a perfunctory good-bye, and rushed from the room.

* * *

"She says somethin' about Fallon being facilitative or somesuch. I says, 'That's it?' And she says, 'What else is there?'"

"What you have to understand," Ronald Carpenter said with a knowing nod, "is that HR people see themselves as, first and foremost, 'people people.' They see themselves as keepers of the organization's spiritual flame while everyone else goes about the crass, grubby business of business. As a result, they often tend to be liked but are not particularly well respected— at least not for their contributions to the bottom line. They tend to be viewed as a necessary evil as opposed to being *real* contributors to the cause. And you know what?"

"What?" Gatling replied.

"It drives them crazy," Carpenter said. "More than anything, they want to have a seat at the grown-ups' table. They want to be viewed as being in the mainstream of the business rather than as the people you go to when you run out of claim forms for your dental insurance. That's why they're always running off to conferences with themes such as 'The HR Professional as Strategic Asset' or 'HR: The Last Untapped Resource.' They spend a couple of days talking to each other and crying on each other's shoulders. And believe me: There's a *lot* of crying—or at least hugging—that goes on at such meetings. And then they come back full of ideas and action plans. That's when they're at their most dangerous."

"How so?" Gatling asked.

"They come back all fired up about programs such as 'participative management' or '360-degree feedback' or 'the power of Empowerment' and they make the rest of the management team—the ones who are up to their hips in the *real* business of the business—crazy. You hear line managers saying things such as, 'I already got plenty of croutons on my salad. I don't need some tree-hugging hold-over from the sixties loading me up with any more.'"

"But," Gatling said, hardly believing that he was about to say what he was about to say, "isn't this Empowerment stuff good? Don't you *want* to get all you can get outta your people?"

"Of course you do, but Empowerment isn't the way to go. Of all of the Next Big Things that have come along over the past ten, fifteen years, Empowerment may be the most suspect one of all."

"Why so?"

"Because Empowerment is really condescension masquerading as inclusion."

"You wanna run that one by me again?"

"Look. Let's say I'm your boss. And one day I say that I'm going to 'empower you' to do a better job, or to take more initiative, or to embrace a new set of challenges, or whatever. That might sound like a show of faith or confidence in you, but at a gut level there's something about it that doesn't feel quite right. After all, you're a fully functioning adult. You own your own home. You balance your own checkbook. You're allowed to vote. You're allowed to marry. You're allowed to procreate. And I tell you that I'm going to give you some 'power'—as though it were mine to give in the first place. Because my name is in a box above yours on some sort of organizational chart, all of a sudden I'm a hydroelectric plant?"

"People actually say that?"

"No, and that's my point. 'Empowerment' sounds so right that it's dangerous. In their gut, people sense that it's just a lot of management woo-woo. They're being treated like children and they don't realize it—at least not on a conscious level. Or if they do, they're smart enough not to say so."

The haze was beginning to lift for Gatling.

"Even if that's all true," Gatling said, "what's it got to do with Carol Thomas and how she felt about what Fallon was doing?"

"The point," Carpenter said, "is that whereas people sensed that Empowerment was just a lot of management woo-woo, they also sensed that CVC was the real deal. It didn't condescend to them and say, 'We are going to deign to bestow the power upon you.' It said, 'We recognize that you already have the power, you already have the answers, and we need to hear them from you.' In the final analysis, it made the HR function—Carol Thomas—look bad, ineffectual. It marginalized their contribution even further than it had been traditionally.

When all is said and done, her approach amounted to encouraging people to feel not to think, and in their heart of hearts, people know that that's not enough. At least it's not enough for grown-ups."

"Well," Gatling shrugged, "the way I see it, Michael Fallon ain't gonna be doing much of either, thinking *or* feeling, I mean."

"No," Carpenter said, somberly, "I guess he, uh, isn't."

CHAPTER 8

ALL HAIL-FELLOW well-met, John Salinsky had yet to see a big idea he couldn't claim to embrace or a little detail he couldn't manage to drop. As Lodestar's VP of Sales & Marketing, he viewed corporate staffers as "those weenies who spend the money that me and my guys are out here bustin' our keisters to make." He saw NBT programs as the embodiment of just that kind of corporate wastefulness, but he was also politically savvy enough to know the difference between jumping on a bandwagon and throwing yourself under the wheels of one as it rolled by. In fact, Salinsky had driven a Lodestar Next Big Thing bandwagon himself—Customer Focus—until it had run out of gas a few years earlier.

"John Salinsky," Salinsky said brightly, a bowling ball of a man rolling across Meeting Room III at The Wayne House, offering his hand in introduction with his customary unctuous bonhomie.

"Lieutenant Gatling," he said, shaking Salinsky's hand and motioning for him to be seated.

"Thanks much," Salinsky said. "And before we go any further, let me save you some time. Between five and six o'clock I had a telephone attached to my ear. I'm a sales guy. That's what I do. I talk to customers. And when I'm not talking to customers, I'm thinking about talking to customers. And when I'm not thinking about talking to customers, I'm thinking about why I'm not thinking about talking to customers. Anyway, I heard from the others that that's the first question you asked—'Where were you between five and six o'clock?'—so I figured I could add a little value to the conversation by saving you the bother of asking."

"Thanks," Gatling replied, out of breath from the mere act of listening to Salinsky.

"Don't mention it. It's who I am. It's what I do."

Actually, Salinsky's opening fusillade *had* saved some time. It had given Gatling an opening to get right to the heart of the matter.

"You said," Gatling began, "you wanted to add a little value to our conversation. I get that right?"

"Right as rain, chief."

"Fallon ever say anything to you about something called the Value Effect?"

"No, don't think so. Not that I can recall."

"Did he do that?" Gatling asked, moving on. "Did Fallon add a little value to Lodestar?"

"No, Mikey Fallon didn't add a little value to Lodestar," Salinsky replied. "Mikey Fallon added a *lot* of value to Lodestar. And I don't say that lightly."

"How come?"

"Because—and I'm bein' brutally honest here—nine times out of ten, we start a new NBT, and I tell all my guys, I tell 'em, 'You guys know the drill: BOHICA.'"

"Wha'?"

"'BOHICA: Bend over. Here it comes again!' It means that some corporate staff type with a little too much time on her hands—and I know I'm not supposed to say 'her,' I'm supposed to say 'their,' but for one thing, that ain't grammatical, and for another thing, it usually *is* a her. So like I was sayin', some corporate type with a little too much time on 'their' hands cooks up some new damn program and we all gotta pay attention to it instead of talking to customers or thinking about talking to customers. So, instead of doing our real work, we have to, you know, BOHICA."

"What you're telling me is when you worked with Fallon, you didn't have to, uh, bend over?"

"You got it, chief. When Mikey talked about CVC—and to be perfectly honest, I don't give a rat's patootie whether you called it 'CVC' or 'Delores,' if you know what I mean—but when Mikey talked about CVC he was talking about opening up a line of sight to the customer for everybody in the company. And I'm not talking about any of this 'internal customer' crap, either. The way I figure it, I ain't the internal customer of the HR department—at least not 'til I can decide to take my HR business to *another* HR department. Far as I'm concerned, customers are 'people who decide to give us their money even though they got other options.' CVC is all about getting everybody in the company to understand more about who has the money and what we have to do to get them to give it to us."

"And that's a big deal?"

"Big? It's so big it's 'uge! I mean, I'm a sales and marketing guy, and any sales and marketing guy I know would give his left one to get everybody else thinking that way. I know, I know. I did it again. But I couldn't exactly say 'give his *or her*' left one 'cause that wouldn't make no sense at all, now would it?"

"Hold on—gimme a second . . . ," Gatling said, holding up his left hand as a temporary stop sign as he tried to keep up with his note taking.

"Take your time, chief," Salinsky replied. "No problem at all."

It took Gatling about thirty more seconds before he was ready to move on.

"You mentioned programs," he began again. "Didn't Lodestar have some kinda Customer Focus program a while ago? Didn't you head it up?"

"Absolutely," Salinsky said.

"Successful?"

"Depends on how you define 'successful.' If by successful you mean it got everybody in the company to resonate—that's one of them new words it's good to toss around now and then: 'resonate.' Kinda like the way Mikey would throw around 'align' and 'energize.' Anyway, if you mean it got everybody to resonate to the customer then, no, it didn't do that. Between you and me, that's not what I was tryin' to do."

"It wasn't?"

"No, it wasn't."

"Then what were you trying to do?"

"BOLIFOB."

"BOLIFOB?"

"BOLIFOB: 'Bend over. Let it fly on by.' I mean, Bill Tollikson—God bless him, he's a prince of a guy—but he was driving us crazy with a new NBT every year. You know: BOHICA. So I figured, if we're going to have to have another new Next Big Thing, I might as well put myself in a position where it could do the least damage. So by being in a position to run the damn thing, I was able to say to my guys—sorry: my *gals* and guys— 'Don't worry. You go about doing your jobs. You know. The stuff that actually brings money *into* the company. I'll be back here makin' sure that it doesn't get in your way.' So, my instruction to them was, in a word, 'BOLIFOB.'"

"Kinda cynical, wouldn't you say?" Gatling asked.

"Hey," Salinsky countered, for the first time showing just a trace of frustration. "I got a job to do and part of that job is making sure that these Next Big Things don't get in the way of little things, like selling products and making money. I don't call that cynical. I call that practical."

"But CVC wasn't getting in the way."

"Not at all. What it was doing was what I've been trying to get this organization to do for years. I'm not too proud to say that Mikey was just flat out better at it than I was. What he was good at was betting buy-in. Without him, it'll be a lot harder to get through to all the people in this company who forget where their paychecks come from. CVC will be a harder sale to make. I'm not sure even I can make it, and I'm a pretty damn good closer."

* * *

"Salinsky," Ronald Carpenter said as he entered Meeting Room III for the post-Salinsky-interrogation debriefing session. "He's the Sales and Marketing guy, right?"

"Right," Gatling said.

"Let me guess. I'll bet he told you something along the lines of, 'CVC is just what I've been trying to instill in this company for years.' Am I right?"

Gatling nodded.

"And I'll bet he also said something like, 'What Sales and Marketing person *wouldn't* go for something like CVC? It's what we do. It's why we're here.' Maybe even, 'It's who we are.' Am I right again?"

"Yeah, pretty much, yeah," Gatling said.

"So, you figure, 'Why wouldn't someone in Salinsky's position want something like CVC to be a big success?'"

"Right again."

"Exactly! He did to you what he does best. He sold you. He charmed you. That's what Sales and Marketing guys are. They're professional charmers."

"How so? I mean, I'm as skeptical as the next guy," Gatling said. "You gotta be in this line of work, but why wouldn't CVC be helpful to a guy like Salinsky? Wouldn't it support what sales and marketing types gotta do?"

Carpenter's reply was emphatic. "No, no, no, no, no! CVC couldn't be more different from what's traditionally involved in sales and marketing. It involves putting different people in front of customers, trying to get at different kinds of information. It involves asking customers different kinds of questions."

"So?"

"So, you've gotta keep in mind that sales and marketing types are very protective and territorial about 'their' customers. I'll bet he snuck in a shot or two about how he and his guys are out there making money while the corporate types back at headquarters are the ones spending it. Am I right? Didn't he?"

"Pretty much."

"Sales types can get pretty self-righteous and sancti-monious about that stuff. And sales management types often succeed by setting up an 'us versus them' mentality: 'You guys just go out and do your jobs. I'll be back here holding the Philistines at bay.'"

"BOLIFOB," Gatling muttered, under his breath.

"Excuse me?" Carpenter asked.

"Never mind," Gatling said, once again impressed by Carpenter's insightfulness.

"Let me guess," Carpenter said. "Salinsky never heard of the Value Effect either, right?"

"Right."

"Again, it figures," Carpenter said, shaking his head.

Gatling was still puzzled about a basic question. "Even if everything you say is true, wasn't what Fallon was doing helpful to Salinsky?" he asked.

"Yes, but Salinsky didn't see it. All he saw was Michael's charm and easy manner. He didn't see the substance of what Michael was doing, because he's a sales guy. He thinks charm and an easy manner *are* substance. The trouble with Salinsky is that once CVC began to be felt and understood, people would have been asking questions such as, 'Why haven't we been doing these things all along?' and 'Who's been responsible for the old ways of doing them?' Salinsky had a lot to lose from CVC. It made him look bad, incompetent. Worse, it brought out the kind of ugly territorial impulses that make traditional sales and marketing guys good at the traditional ways of selling and marketing. Trouble is, there isn't anything traditional about what Michael Fallon is selling to them."

"No," Gatling corrected him. "There ain't anything traditional about what Michael Fallon *was* selling to them."

"Point well taken," Carpenter said, with grim resignation.

CHAPTER 9

DARREN HATFIELD was the kind of chief financial officer who, even in these enlightened times, embodied 1960s-style command-and-control, rule-by-fear management. Known unofficially as "The Brow" for the four-inch-long black caterpillar that seemed to nestle over his eyes whenever he squinted in judgment at what anyone else might have to say, Hatfield saw himself as the ultimate rational man: If you couldn't measure it—preferably in dollars—then it didn't really exist. He thought that all of the Next Big Things tried by Lodestar over the years had been exactly equivalent, that is, utterly worthless.

So, when Lenny Gatling asked Hatfield his customary, "Where were you between five and six o'clock?" opening question, he got the full brow treatment. Hatfield rolled the question over in his mind for a couple of seconds before deigning to answer, and then fixed Gatling with the kind of disdainful stare usually reserved for food stuffs that have been left in the back of the refrigerator for too long.

"What I *wasn't* doing was murdering Michael Fallon, if that's what you're driving at," he began. "What I *was* doing was answering my phone messages. Much as I hate to let real business intrude on one of our all-important off-site man-agement circle jerks, sometimes you just have no choice."

"Who were you talking to? Whose messages were you returning?"

"Two separate calls. Both to securities analysts. Some-body's got to cater to these guys so that our stock price is high enough that we can raise enough money to pay for these little soirees that we have so often."

"Those two calls, they filled up the hour?" Gatling asked.

"Most of it," Hatfield replied, the brow seeming to thicken by a millimeter or two. "Maybe up until about five-forty-five, five-fifty, or so. Then I went down to the lobby."

"You didn't have to be in the lobby until six o'clock, right?

"No," Hatfield replied, condescendingly. "The cars were going to leave for the restaurant at six o'clock, but I had to be there earlier."

"Why?"

"Because I had gotten wind of a meeting that Carol Thomas was going to have with Bill Tollikson about some sort of new associates benefits package. I heard them talking about it during one of the coffee breaks today."

"Why'd you need to be involved in that?" Gatling asked.

"Because leaving those two together is a dangerous thing to do," Hatfield explained. "I mean, just think of the word: 'associates.' Nice word, I suppose, but somebody has to be daddy and remind people that we aren't an association, we're a business. And the business of business is business, not flex-time and casual Fridays and cafeteria benefits."

"So, you figure you coulda added something to the conversation they were having?"

"No. I figured that I could *stop* the conversation they were having. I knew that as soon as they saw me get off the elevator and start walking toward them, they would stop."

"It work?"

"Beautifully," Hatfield said. "Sometimes the best offense is a good defense, know what I mean?"

"I s'pose," Gatling said.

"Beautifully," Hatfield repeated, savoring the memory, relaxed enough now that the brow actually broke in two for a brief instant.

"So," Gatling said, recapturing control of the interrogation, "tell me about Fallon."

"What about Fallon?"

"Was he good for Lodestar? Bad for Lodestar? Somewhere in the middle?"

The brow actually split a millimeter or two further. "What you gotta understand is that generally speaking, I've got no use at all for consultants. You know that old line about consultants, the one that goes 'A consultant is somebody who will borrow your watch to tell you what time it is'?"

"No," Gatling said.

"Well, it's actually gotten a lot worse than that in recent years," Hatfield continued, characteristically ignoring Gatling's response, as the brow returned to its customary four-inch, one-piece configuration. "At least the old way you'd get some sort of hard result. You'd know what time it was, even though you could have figured it out for yourself easily enough. Today, though, nobody has any answers. Today everything is about process. Today, consultants will borrow your watch, take it apart, then give you advice while you try to put it back together again."

"What's the point of that?" Gatling queried.

"Because that way they know you'll have to ask them to come back when you get the watch back together because there's always a piece left over, and besides which, it doesn't keep very good time anymore. Consultants are very good at keeping their eye on the ball, which, in their case, means 'billable hours.' And the way they keep their eye on the ball is to help you take your eyes off yours. You know, get everybody off-site 'sharing' with each other instead of being at their desks doing what they're supposed to be doing, like, say, running the business."

"Does something called the Value Effect ring a bell with you? Fallon ever talk about that with you?"

"No," Hatfield said. "Then again, I never exactly went out of my way to chit chat with him." The brow thickened above a malevolently self-satisfied grin.

"Let's back up to my original question," Gatling pressed. "Fallon. Good for Lodestar? Bad for Lodestar?"

Hatfield actually gave a slight chuckle as he reconsidered Gatling's question.

"I mean, I wasn't all that close to the projects he was working on," he began, chuckling again. "I'm not all that sure of just what it was that he actually *did* on them, but I guess, all things considered, Michael Fallon was, net, probably pretty good for Lodestar."

"How do you know?"

"Business reasons," Hatfield replied. "Like, for instance, our costs are down. Our sales are up. We can actually move products to market faster than we ever could. Even—and you've got to understand that I normally wouldn't give a warm fig for things like this, except insofar as they help us get our sales up and our costs down and our products to market faster—even employee morale is up."

"But you've had a bunch of other NBTs over the years," Gatling said. "You've done all this kinda stuff before, no?"

Hatfield rolled his eyes. "Oh, yeah," he said, "we've had all kinds of nice programs. And about the only good thing that I can say about them is that when you have one of those kinds of NBT programs going on, you have to have a lot of meetings. Kind of like this one. And although the people who believe in those sorts of NBT programs are off at meetings like this one, that means that they aren't back at the office getting in other people's way. That's about it, as far as I can say."

"But this one, CVC, was different, you said. You said this one was working," Gatling said.

Hatfield shrugged and nodded resignedly. "Understand that *all* of our NBTs got some results—some not even all that different from what we've gotten with CVC—at least in the short term. Much as it pains me to admit it, I have to give the consultant credit. Maybe he laid it on a little thick with all that business about customer-ness and alignment and energy. But— what the hell—you've got to give him a mulligan or two. I get the sense that this time we'll even be able to hold some of the gains we've made. I'm not too sure exactly what it was he did to make this happen, but, yeah, I guess I have to take my hat off to Fallon."

"Lotta people will be doing that the next few days," Gatling added. "Taking their hats off to Fallon, I mean."

"I'm afraid you're right," Hatfield replied, the brow splitting wide open to reveal a face that, for once, wasn't very stern at all.

* * *

"Oh, puh-leeze, spare me," Ronald Carpenter said when Gatling reported a summary of his just concluded interrogation of Darren Hatfield. "Darren Hatfield, the CFO of Lodestar, said that Michael Fallon—a consultant—was a *good* thing for the company?"

"Yeah," Gatling said, "he did. And he was pretty sure of it, too, even though he was, quote, 'not too sure exactly what it was he did to make this happen.'"

"Look," Carpenter said, shaking his head, "there's one thing you've just got to understand. The CFO is the natural enemy of any consulting effort. The kinds of interventions that Michael was managing with Lodestar take some time, but CFO types want results and they want them yesterday because Wall Street wants them the day before yesterday. I'm not even going to waste the time to ask if he knew anything about the Value Effect, because I already know the answer to that one."

"But Hatfield said Fallon was getting results," Gatling said. "Said that was what made CVC different."

"He might have said that," Carpenter said, "but I promise you he didn't really believe it. In his heart of hearts what he really believes is something more along the lines of, 'Yeah, I suppose Fallon was getting us some results, but it wasn't anything that we couldn't have done ourselves if we spent more time worrying about the business and less time worrying about how involved and fulfilled our associates have become due to the newly participative nature of our corporate culture.'"

"Why would he say that if he didn't believe it?"

Carpenter's eyes widened. "You're the homicide detective and you're asking *me* that question? You've got a dead body next door and you want to know why somebody might have *lied* to you?"

"Yeah, yeah. I get your point," Gatling answered. "With the others, you said they had a motive to do away with Fallon. You said that Fallon's success with CVC was making them all look bad because all of them screwed the pooch when they ran their own Next Big Thing. But Hatfield didn't run a Next Big Thing. And the results of CVC made him look good with the people he cared about, like stock analysts and guys on the board of directors and themsuch. So, yeah, why would he lie?"

Carpenter smiled a mischievous smile. "I think you've put your finger on it, my sleuthful friend," he said.

"How so?" Gatling asked.

"You've got to consider the politics of this thing. Lodestar has been trying one NBT after another for the past several years. None of them has worked, right? Or at least none of them lived up to their own hype, right?"

"Right. Least that's what Hatfield said."

"Right. That's what Hatfield said. Who is the only Lodestar vice president whose reputation hasn't been compromised by the failure of one of these Next Big Things?"

"Hatfield?"

"Right, Hatfield. Now, what do you suppose was the patience level of the people who Hatfield cared about— securities analysts and the board of directors—with these Next Big Things?"

"Pretty low?"

"Correct. Now, last question. Each of those other VPs was identified with one NBT, but who was the one person who was tied to *all* of them?"

"I dunno," Gatling offered. "Tollikson maybe?"

"Bingo!" Carpenter enthused. "When all was said and done, Bill Tollikson was the one who had everybody flitting from one Next Big Thing to the next. Bill Tollikson was the one who was paying all of those big consultant bills. Bill Tollikson was the one who was keeping the rest of the company from keeping their eye on the ball. And Darren Hatfield was the only one who was consistent in his opposition to *all* of those Next Big Things.

"So," Carpenter said, with the look of a man who had just snapped the last piece of a Rubik's Cube neatly into place, "what do you suppose might have happened if this latest Next Big Thing—CVC—had failed?"

The light began to dawn for Gatling. "What you're saying is, if CVC fails, it's the last straw for Tollikson."

"Right. And?" Carpenter prompted.

"In the eyes of the two kinds of people who Hatfield sucked up to—stockholders and the board of directors—the logical guy to replace Tollikson woulda been Hatfield."

"Game, set, and match!" Carpenter beamed. "And a hard-ass like Hatfield, he'd have walked over a dead body to become CEO!"

"And my guess," Gatling added, "he wouldn't be wearing tennis shoes, either."

CHAPTER 10

CEO BILL TOLLIKSON was universally admired as a good and kind man who deeply wanted what was right for Lodestar and its people. That was his motive for having everyone in the company move with vigor from Next Big Thing to Next Big Thing over the past five years. After a strong start, however, each NBT had petered out. Moreover, people increasingly had a hard time seeing just how all of these programs fit together. So, sadly, instead of beeing seen as resourceful and action-oriented, Tollikson was regarded as feckless and irresolute, adjectives not generally appearing at the top of most people's lists of key leadership attributes.

His unprepossessing physical appearance did not make matters any better. In an altogether too appropriate statistical quirk, both his height and his weight were precisely at the national average for men of his age. And his wardrobe was remarkable only for its unremarkability. "I've never seen anyone who could make a gray suit seem so unexciting," Betty Bradford once said of Tollikson, with the kind of ironic affection that perfectly captured his relationship with the Lodestar executive team. But to even think that Bill Tollikson would be capable of doing the sort of thing that had been done to Michael Fallon was, well, unthinkable. Then again, pretty much everything about what Lenny Gatling did for a living was pretty much unthinkable when you got right down to it. So, he didn't have any more than the usual hesitation when he asked his standard opening question of Lodestar's CEO.

"Where were you between five and six o'clock this evening?"

More so than any of the others, Tollikson was taken aback by the question.

"Surely, Lieutenant," he began, indignation rising, "you don't think I had anything to do with Michael Fallon's murder, do you?"

"Well, Mr. Tollikson," Gatling replied, "it's like this. I'm not making any judgments. That's for judges. I'm a detective, so what I gotta do is detect. And because Fallon's wearin' a toe tag, I probably ain't gonna get a lotta answers outta him. So, I gotta do the next best thing, which means that I gotta ask everybody else some questions. And seeing as how you're part of everybody else, I guess I gotta ask you, too."

"I suppose you do," Tollikson said, somewhat mollified.

"So," Gatling repeated, "where were you during that hour?"

"I went back to my room and called my wife," Tollikson said, proudly adding, "I've been traveling on business for more than forty years, and I've been away from home a lot of nights, but there isn't a single one of those nights that I didn't call and talk to my wife."

"How long did you talk to her?"

"Ten, fifteen minutes. Just enough to catch up, see how her day had gone. Tell her I love her. That sort of thing."

"So, that takes us to about five-fifteen," Gatling said, blowing right past the sentimentality of Tollikson's response. "Then what'd you do? Check your voice mail messages?"

"No," Tollikson said, with a pinch of disdain. "Those infernal things could wait until later. Everybody thinks that their message is so earth-shatteringly important that it has to be responded to *right now!* Over the years I've come to realize that things move along at their own pace and that you can affect that pace and not have your message machine rule your day."

"OK," Gatling replied. "That's how you didn't use the rest of that hour. How *did* you use it?"

"I spent a few minutes reading through some of the materials that Carol Thomas sent me. She and I were to meet in the lobby at five-thirty to go over some of her ideas about a new benefits package that we're considering offering our associates, and I wanted to be ready for that discussion."

"So, you went down to the lobby at five-thirty?"

"Yes. Maybe a couple of minutes before."

"Met with Carol Thomas?"

"Yes. She and I were talking. Actually, we ended our meeting when Darren Hatfield happened to get off the elevator and stopped by to chat. Then we heard the terrible news about Michael," Tollikson said. He closed his eyes and gave two small shakes of his head.

Gatling respectfully allowed the silence to settle between them for a moment or two before pressing on with his questioning.

"Speaking of Fallon," he said, "what'd you think of him?"

Tollikson paused. Under the circumstances, this simple question bordered on the overwhelming for him. He chose his words carefully. "Michael was a good man. Very careful. Very thorough, precise. He always said that he liked to do things exactly right, and even though we kidded him a lot about it, he usually did."

Tollikson smiled, then looked down at his hands. He took a deep breath before adding: "He did us a lot of good. And he will be missed."

"Just how did he do you a lot of good?"

"By helping us with CVC." Tollikson smiled again, sadly. "Whenever I thought about CVC, I thought, *Finally we're getting it right.*"

"Why finally?"

"It's not that the specific things we're doing—the actual steps we're taking with CVC—are all that different from things we've done with past NBTs. CVC has elements of all of them in it," Tollikson said. "And the hard, measurable results we've been getting with CVC—efficiency, productivity, time-to-market . . . those sorts of things—they've been good, but not remarkably better than the kinds of results we've gotten in the past . . . at least not as far as short-term results go."

Gatling was puzzled. "You're telling me that you're taking the same kinds of steps, and you've gotten the same kinds of results . . . but you're saying that CVC is working significantly better? Maybe I'm missing something, but that don't seem to make sense."

Tollikson gave a small, rueful smile. "Welcome to the club," he said. "I'd say pretty much the same thing to Michael all the time: 'It doesn't make sense that this is working better. It isn't logical!'" He gave a small shrug of bafflement. "But for some reason, it has been. For some reason, we've gotten better buy-in . . . people are more aligned. They seem to be more motivated to accept change, more energized to keep at it."

Without looking up from his note taking, Gatling asked: "Ever hear of something called the Value Effect?"

"The Value Effect?" Tollikson mulled the question. "No. I can't say that I have. Why?"

"No big deal," Gatling said, waving Tollikson's concern away. "Just something I heard about. Something you said made me think of it." He looked up from his notes. "I'm sorry, I interrupted. You were saying?"

Tollikson paused and shook his head before continuing.

"You try to be rational," he said. "Analytical. Data driven. Fact based. You try to do things that make sense. You know: pay attention to the hard stuff. The 'real' stuff. And then it's the soft stuff that gets you. Happens every time. Maybe we've finally learned our lesson. It sure as hell has been a painful one to learn."

"Not as painful as the one Fallon learned."

"No," Tollikson reflected. "I don't suppose it is."

* * *

"Do you want to know why the earlier NBTs failed?" Carpenter's question was more of a challenge than an inquiry.

"Sure. Why?" Gatling responded.

"It's like the old joke about why dogs . . . Well, never mind that. The fact of the matter is that they failed because they *could* fail."

"I'm not followin'."

"Look at it this way: You're a VP at Lodestar. Your boss, Tollikson, tells you he wants you to be the head honcho of this year's Next Big Thing. You know enough to salute smartly and say yes. If you didn't, you never would have made VP in the first place. Now you're in charge of something that you're not sure you really believe in, and you'd just as soon not be bothered with it at all. After all, you've got all you can handle to do your real work without having to take on Bill Tollikson's latest wet dream of a corporate initiative. You with me?"

"Keep goin'," Gatling said.

"Basically, then, you've got two choices. You can really go all out, put in a lot of time and effort to really do it right, to really get everyone in the organization behind it . . . to buy into what you're trying to do. Keep in mind that in your spare time—nights, weekends, holidays—you still have your real job responsibilities to attend to. You're not off the hook from those. Or you can just make a good show of it. You can do the safe, obvious things. You can print the posters, hold the meetings, give out the little lucite mementos at management meetings, and basically let the NBT die a nice, peaceful death. And what would the result of that be?"

"You tell me."

"You'd have the Next Big Thing off your back, you could get back to your real job, and somebody else would have to take on the *next* Next Big Thing. It would have been *their* turn in the barrel. You talked to Magliori and Bradford and Thomas and Salinsky. Did they seem particularly scarred by the failures of their NBTs?"

"No," Gatling said, thinking back, "now that you mention it."

"Exactly. They failed because they *could* fail. There were no consequences. In fact, they were better off having the monkey off their back and onto somebody else's. Any way you slice it, though, the bottom line is that all the failed NBTs of the past years happened on Tollikson's watch. It might have been his VPs who were responsible for those failed programs, but even still, the buck stops with the CEO."

"But why would Tollikson wanna get rid of Fallon," Gatling asked. "I mean, one of his Next Big Things was finally working."

"True enough, but Michael's success at leading people toward a goal—at creating alignment and energy—was shining a pretty bright light on Tollikson's shortcomings. And those shortcomings are at the heart of what a CEO is supposed to do . . . what a CEO is supposed to *be*. Maybe Tollikson figured that failing at yet another program is bad, but being guilty of a gross failure of leadership could be fatal." Carpenter paused.

He shook his head, unsure of whether he really believed what he heard himself saying. "I don't know. That sounds a little convoluted to me. A little crazy."

"Maybe, but you know what?" Gatling asked.

"No, what?"

"There's crazy people in the world. 'Specially the world I live in."

CHAPTER 11

LENNY GATLING was sitting, alone, in Meeting Room III of The Wayne House. Although Ronald Carpenter had left nearly an hour earlier, Gatling found himself still reflecting on the last thing Condor's CEO had said to him: "It must be tough to live in the world you live in."

Gatling knew that most people would be amazed to hear that the tough part of his world had nothing to do with the sordid parts of the job—the brutality and the mayhem and whatnot. (After you've been in homicide for twenty-two years, words such as *brutality* and *mayhem* fit perfectly with *whatnot.*)

No, the tough part was the frustration he felt when the pieces wouldn't fall into place for him.

He leaned back in his chair, closed his eyes, and took in a deep breath. He let it out in a slow, steady stream.

What have I missed? he asked himself.

Physical evidence? So far, his forensics guys had turned up nothing.

Clues back at Lodestar headquarters? Again, nothing yet.

What the suspects said? Sure, there were leads to follow up, but nothing very dramatic had come from the initial round of interrogations.

What have I missed?

It was late, and he was tired, and what compounded his frustration was the fact that he knew—deep in his bones—that a short while ago he had sat alone in a room with a stone cold killer . . . and that he knew—deep in his soul—that the thing that would make all the pieces fall into place for him, the critical bit of information that seemed so elusive right now, would turn out to have been right under his nose all along. Mocking him. Daring him to find it.

He got up from his chair and began to walk slowly toward the door of Meeting Room III. Had you asked him why or where he was going, he would have said that he didn't know. What he did know was that he shouldn't ask himself those questions. He knew enough to trust his instincts and let them take him wherever they were inclined to take him.

This time they took him down the hallway toward Meeting Room II. He entered, nodded to his colleagues guarding the crime scene, and began to walk slowly around the perimeter of the room.

He walked. Then he walked some more. And as he did this, he let all of the information he had about the case wash over him. After a bit, he stopped walking. He wasn't sure why.

What am I missing?

He stared, blankly, at the wall directly across the room. One of the flip charts from the Lodestar meeting was still taped to it. It was the one with Monday's agenda.

In the next moment he found himself standing directly in front of that wall, staring—hard—at the agenda.

Aha! he thought. ***This** is what I'm s'posed to see!*

He wheeled, strode out of Meeting Room II, and quickly covered the twenty-five feet to the entrance of Meeting Room III. Throwing the door open, he barreled toward the stack of papers that was still sitting on the table next to the chair from which he had conducted the interrogations of the seven suspects in Fallon's murder.

He found Fallon's Value Effect memo in the stack. Looking at its first page, he smiled, sat down, and began to read. The pieces, he was now quite confident, would soon be falling into place. Lenny Gatling still didn't know who had killed Fallon, but he knew that by the time he finished reading, there would be just one name left on his list.

The
Solution

CHAPTER 12

"THANK YOU all for coming."

That Lenny Gatling would begin with such a slight, trivial amenity struck the others as odd. Particularly given where they were. Particularly given why they were there. Particularly given the fact that his 6:30 a.m. calls summoning them to this 7:00 a.m. meeting had not made it sound as though attendance were in any sense optional.

Under the circumstances, Gatling's opening words seemed a bit too polite, and the incongruity added to the tension and anxiety that was already flowing thick in Meeting Room II of The Wayne House.

This was exactly the effect that Lenny Gatling intended.

Nothing had been moved. (This was, after all, still a murder scene.) The seats were in the same U-shaped arrangement they had been in the day before. And as people tend to do, they had all taken exactly the same seats they had occupied yesterday. The seat that had been occupied by Michael Fallon—the one at the top of the left upright of the U—remained poignantly empty.

Gatling had been standing at the top of the U when he spoke his five simple words of greeting. For several moments, those remained the only words he spoke, as he proceeded to pace, slowly and quietly. Back and forth across the front of the room. Up and down inside the U. Back and forth. Up and down. Seven sets of eyes following this metronomic pattern.

The tension rose. (Lenny Gatling was good at what he did.) When, finally, Gatling stopped and spoke again, it was in soft, measured tones.

"I talked to each of you last night," he said. "I know that was a hard thing for you to do, and I wanna thank you for, ya know, overcoming that difficulty and giving me your time."

Impatient fidgets. *Enough already with the etiquette! When is he going to get down to it?*

Gatling let this go on, just so, before continuing.

"And Mr. Carpenter here," he said, "served as my guide, my translator, my—whatchallit?" He looked to Ronald Carpenter for the answer.

"Your shadow consultant," Carpenter said.

"Yeah, that's it," Gatling said. "And I wanna thank you for doin' that. It was very helpful."

Carpenter gave him an acknowledging nod.

"One reason it was especially helpful is because I'm not a businessman. I'm a cop. I walk into one of these sophisticated business meetings like you got goin' on here, and—" Gatling stopped pacing and gave a broad shrug. "I'm kinda outta my element. You guys are all comfortable with all of this stuff about Focused Customer Quality and Reengineered Empowerment and all of the other NBTs you guys deal with. Isn't that what you call them?"

They all nodded.

"Yeah, well, I know this sounds like a terrible thing to say, but—" Gatling swept both arms to encompass all of Meeting Room II. "I'm comfortable around a murder scene." His expression was half matter-of-fact, half apologetic.

"The way I figure it," Gatling continued, "my guess is that my job—catching bad guys—seems like it's pretty complicated. You probably figure you don't understand my business just like I figure I don't understand yours.

"Let me try to explain. I think I might have already explained this to some of you. But for the others . . . in a nutshell, here's my job. I start with a list of people who might have done it. I look around. See what there is to see. Ask some questions. Pretty soon, I start crossing names off the list. And when there's just one name left—badda-bing, badda-boom—I'm done."

He said this as though it involved all the complexity of affixing a stamp to a letter. The mood in Meeting Room II turned that much more chilling. (Lenny Gatling was *very* good at what he did.)

"Anyway, I made up my initial list." He held up his note-book as a visual aid. "It had seven names on it." Even though the writing in the notebook was much too small for any of them to be able to read, all seven of them got the gist of what Gatling was saying. The chill factor went down another notch. More fidgets.

"In other words . . ." He paused for two beats. "You folks."

There were audible gasps. Of course, everyone had long since realized that they were all suspects, but to hear it said out loud gave that supposition a terrifying validity.

"Sorry for being so blunt, folks," Gatling said, "but, you know, homicide ain't bean bag. There's just no nice way to do this. So I'm just gonna do it.

"Generally speaking, there's three things somebody's gotta have before they're gonna kill somebody else. First, they've gotta have the means. Well, we all know what the means were. The tchotchkes. And, hell, if there's anybody who had access to those, it was all of you guys, no? I mean, you've been doing this CVC thing for about a year now, haven't you? And you've all got the posters and the mugs and the bumper stickers and all the rest, don't you?"

They were all frozen silent.

"Well?" Gatling pressed. "Don't you?"

It was Bill Tollikson who spoke. "Yes, sir," he said. "We do. Except maybe for Mr. Carpenter."

All eyes shifted to Ronald Carpenter.

"I wish I could agree with Mr. Tollikson," Carpenter said. "But Michael always had samples of those kinds of things around his office. He always said it helped to keep him connected to his clients."

"That was very honest and honorable of you, Mr. Carpenter," Gatling said, nodding admiringly. "I also happen to know that it's true, because some of my guys already checked out Fallon's office." Carpenter returned the nod.

Gatling continued. "So, you all had the means. And, speaking of means, that means I can't cross any names off my list." As he said this, he pulled his right hand—the one holding the pen—away from his notepad, and shook his head slowly, disappointed.

"Next," Gatling said, "comes opportunity. Like I said, I talked to each of you, and it turns out each of you was alone for a significant chunk of time between five and six o'clock last evening. At least a half hour. You all said you were making phone calls. I got no reason not to believe that. Even if I did, it's easy enough to check phone records.

"You know, though, cell phones move. I mean, that's their whole point, ain't it? So, the killer coulda been making calls while walking down the hallway to this very room. Hell, the killer coulda been *on* a call, *during* the murder, *in* this very room. I mean, there's lots of time when you're not talking to an actual human person while you're on voice mail, no? You're just hearing a recorded voice and pushing buttons. A call coulda been made like that, and Fallon . . . well, he coulda paid a helluva roaming charge for it.

"That means that, far as I'm concerned, you all had the opportunity. And that don't do me any good, because I still can't cross any names off my list."

Gatling began his silent pacing again. Back and forth across the front of the room. Up and down inside the U. He did this for twenty-five, thirty, thirty-five excruciating seconds.

He stopped pacing and spoke again. "All I got left is motive. So I ask myself, 'Which of you had a motive to kill Fallon?' And I figure there's just one possible answer."

Again, gasps. Each wanted to look at the others to spot some telltale look or expression. Each was afraid to do so, for fear of looking anxious, suspicious.

"Cool your jets," Gatling said, calmly. "It ain't what you're thinking. The one possible answer I came up with was 'all seven of you,' and that don't do me much good because, well, you know . . ." He again held up his notebook and his pen and gave a resigned shrug.

"I mean, all of you vice presidents who had your own NBT. You worked hard. You did your best. But Fallon—with CVC—he did better. Especially with what everybody's calling the soft stuff. He made you look bad. Bad enough to kill him?"

Gatling paused and gave an exaggerated shrug.

"Who knows?" he said. "Except, of course, maybe one of you."

The four NBT VPs—Magliori, Bradford, Salinsky, Thomas— shifted uneasily in their chairs.

"And Mr. Tollikson," Gatling continued. "You're the big cheese. Ultimately, you were responsible for all the NBTs. You might have had the same motive, but in spades."

Now it was Tollikson's turn to shift in his chair.

"Then we come to Mr. Hatfield, who might have had his— How shall I put this?—political reasons to do Fallon in." He looked at Hatfield, his arched eyebrows asking the question.

Hatfield glowered.

"And Mr. C," Gatling said, turning toward Ronald Carpenter. "Here, you're the one who *invented* CVC." He turned to the others. "Did everybody know that? It was Mr. C here, not Fallon, who was the inventor of CVC?"

The others registered surprise.

"See that?" Gatling asked Carpenter. "How's that make you feel, him getting all the credit for something that was your idea?"

Carpenter's expression was dismissive.

Gatling paced some more. Mulled some more.

After a few moments, Gatling stopped and said to no one in particular, "See, my trouble is that after all of this, I still got seven names on my list. I look at my notes some more . . . read through them one more time to see what you guys all said to me . . . to see if there's anything I missed." Brandishing his notebook, he flipped through the pages here and there. "For example, Mr. Magliori . . . you said that Fallon was 'a good guy.' That he certainly was 'capable' and 'competent.' That 'he knew what he was doing.' In fact, that's pretty much what you all said about Fallon, no?"

Everyone nodded.

"*Very* capable. *Very* competent," Carpenter asserted.

More—and stronger—nods.

"OK," Gatling said. "Very capable and competent. I got no beef with that." He riffled through several more pages. "And

Ms. Bradford, you described Fallon as being 'a good detail man.' I get that right?"

"You did," Bradford replied, her smile signaling gratitude toward Gatling for his paraphrasing of what she had really said.

"Mr. Tollikson," Gatling continued, a page flip later. "You said that he was 'extraordinarily reliable.'"

"Yes, I did," Tollikson said. "In fact, before we started here this morning, I was thinking about the time when Michael's flight got canceled, so he drove all night through a blizzard to make an appointment that he had with me.

"When Michael said that he was going to so something, it would get done. When he said that he was going to be someplace, he would be there." Then he added, with an impossibly sad smile, "You could take it to the bank."

"Hey," Hatfield remembered, "remember the time he *did* take it to the bank? He told me he was going right by the bank on his way home, said he'd make the night deposit for me? But he forgot to stop . . . didn't realize it until he had gotten home . . . all the way out in the suburbs . . . and he drove all the way back into the city that night, even though he was coming back into town first thing the next morning?! That was Fallon. He said he was going to drop it off that night, so he was going to drop it off *that night!*"

Now everyone had that same impossibly sad smile.

"Let's be honest," Thomas said. "Saying that Michael was 'reliable' and 'good with details' is the understatement of the decade. 'Fastidious' is probably a better description. Maybe even 'compulsive.' Sometimes he got a little too wrapped up in making sure that everything was 'exactly right.'"

More nods. More smiles.

"In fact," Thomas continued. "You know the hardest thing for me to believe about what's gone on around here over the past twenty-four hours?"

No one did.

"The fact that we're off schedule. . . off agenda! Michael would never have put up with that!"

"No way!"

"You got that right!"

"Hard to believe!"

This time there was outright laughter. Impossibly sad laughter.

"That's nice that you have such nice stories about Fallon. And it's nice that you all thought well of him," Gatling said before abruptly shifting the mood. "But you know what ain't so nice? The fact that Fallon's gonna be takin' the big dirt nap, and I'm still here with seven names on my list."

Gatling quickened the pace of his pacing.

"I look at all the evidence I got. I look at all the notes I got. I look at all the leads I got. And I feel stuck. You know what I do when that happens?"

No one responded. Gatling continued.

"I go with my gut. I know that ain't particularly scientific. I can't explain how it works. All I know is that it *does* work. Been working for me for twenty-two years, be twenty-three years in June."

They were all riveted. Gatling continued to pace. Up and down the inside of the U. Back and forth across the front of the room.

"And my gut is telling me that something doesn't quite fit. It was just a feeling I had last night, here, in this room, while I was reviewing my notes in my head and the evidence from forensics—it didn't turn up much of anything, by the way: thought you'd like to know. While I was just walking around the room, trying to figure out what it had to say . . . what the room had to say to me. You know the expression: 'If these walls could talk.'?

"I've spent a lot of time in this room, the past two days. I'm pretty familiar with it. Then again, I've found that sometimes, if you look at familiar things from unfamiliar angles you can see things different . . . sometimes even different things. I walked all around this room. Checked it from here. Then from over there. Then from over there.

"So, I look around the walls and, I don't know why, I looked over here at this." He walked to the flip chart taped to the wall to the left of the U. "Fallon's agenda. The one you were supposed to follow. And I remember the reason the words here—CVC: The Bigger Picture—were crossed off. The agenda changed because of this here memo you gave me, didn't it Mr. C?" He held up a thick document.

"Is that the memo about the Value Effect?" Carpenter asked.

"Yeah," Gatling replied.

"Then yes," Carpenter said, nodding. "That's what caused the change to the agenda."

"OK with you if I read out loud some of this memo?" Gatling asked.

"Absolutely," Carpenter said. "By all means."

"Thanks," Gatling continued. He flipped through several pages until he reached the one he was looking for. "Listen to this here. This is kind of interesting. It says—and again, this is Fallon to Mr. Carpenter, right?"

Carpenter nodded. "Yes, that's right."

Gatling continued, "It says that, 'When people strive to deliver the maximum value to customers, they get—and stay— energized.' That's what Fallon called 'the Value Effect.' That's the thing I asked you all about, but nobody had heard of it, right?"

Tentative, wary nods.

Gatling continued, "Fallon goes on to say that the Value Effect is: 'Just a simple, declarative sentence. It's not fancy. It's not complicated. Here's another thing it's not; it's *not* a Next Big Thing. NBTs are sets of tools and techniques and specialized expertise that help an organization deal more effectively with whatever is the issue of the day. The Value Effect, on the other hand, simply "is." It's a fact of human nature. It's a naturally occurring phenomenon, like water flowing downhill, or opposite poles of a magnet attracting, or ice melting when the temperature gets above 32 degrees.'"

Gatling stopped reading for a moment and looked up. "This is pretty interesting stuff, don't you think?"

Only Carpenter showed a noticeable degree of enthusiasm. The others each gave a noncommittal shrug or a muttered "I suppose so" in response.

Gatling continued. "Then he goes on to talk about why it matters so much that this 'Value Effect' thing ain't an NBT. He says, 'Organizations are not made up of automatons. They comprise flesh and blood creatures with moods and emotions and all the rest. . . . When an NBT falls short of its promise . . . people get disappointed. And then another NBT comes along, and a lot of people get disappointed again. As these people make more passes through more cycles of NBTs—as they engage in what might be thought of as "Next Big Thing–ism"—

that disappointment becomes frustration, which eventually decays into the kind of cynicism embodied in references to "the program du jour" and "the flavor of the month," or in the world-weary advice given to the naively enthusiastic: "Don't worry. This too shall pass." And because cynicism sucks energy out of an organization, later NBTs are even less likely to be effective, which breeds still more cynicism, still more frantic attempts to find the *next* Next Big Thing, and the cycle of NBT–ism—an especially vicious, pernicious cycle—continues.'"

"Precisely," Magliori said.

"Bingo," Salinksy said.

"Phriggin' A, Bubba," Bradford said.

"Dead nuts on," Hatfield said.

"What you've just shared with us is 'truth' in its purest, most unadulterated form," Thomas said.

Bill Tollikson was now genuinely excited. "In those few sentences," Tollikson said, shaking his head in morose admiration, "Michael has hit on what's been happening around here for years."

Then he turned to his right to face Ronald Carpenter. "This memo was written to you?" Tollikson asked.

Carpenter nodded.

"Then," he asked, now obviously agitated, "why are we only hearing about the Value Effect now?" It was as much a challenge as it was a question.

Disconcerted, Carpenter fumbled for an instant while trying to frame a response. Gatling came to his rescue.

"Because he didn't know about any of this stuff, either," Gatling said. "He didn't get the memo from Fallon until late Sunday night. Isn't that what you told me, Mr. C? You wanted to share this information with the others on Monday, but it was Fallon who made you wait until Tuesday?"

"Yes," said Carpenter, grateful for having been rescued. He turned and spoke, passionately, to the entire group. "The first time I finished reading the memo that Lieutenant Gatling has been quoting from was Monday morning, about two o'clock. I had the same reaction you've all just had. I was so excited by what Michael had come up with—by this thing he called 'the Value Effect'—that I went directly to his room. I banged on his door. He opened it. I barged in saying, 'This is brilliant. This is what I want to talk about in the meeting tomorrow morning!'

"Michael said that he was glad I felt that way, but he thought we ought to discuss things first. He said that he had begun to get a case of cold feet. He wasn't sure if he was ready to go public with the Value Effect just yet. He was afraid the ideas weren't fully formed. I said, 'We owe it to our client to share this information with them. We can't let the opportunity pass.' We talked about this for quite a while. An hour, maybe an hour and a half. Finally, Michael came up with a compromise. He said, 'OK. You'll talk about the Value Effect, but we'll have you do it on Tuesday morning instead of Monday.' That way, he said he'd have more time to polish it up a little bit.

"He also reminded me that you guys would be deciding the fate of CVC on Monday night. He was sure you were going to give us a thumbs-up for another year of CVC as your NBT. He was afraid that if I talked about the Value Effect on Monday, it would sound like I was trying to lobby you, trying to sell you. So he said, 'Wait until Tuesday. On Monday, just make a few welcoming remarks.' I said, 'That sounds like a plan.' And that was that." And as he said this, Carpenter offered Tollikson a small apologetic shrug.

Tollikson seemed satisfied with Carpenter's explanation.

"Good," Gatling said. "I'm glad that Mr. Carpenter's explanation answered your question. But now let's talk about a question that his explanation *raises*. And it has to do with this."

Gatling walked back over to the flip-charted agenda taped to the wall to the left of the U. And this time his stride was more purposeful and assertive.

"If the decision had been made the night before to move Mr. C's presentation to Tuesday," he said, his voice now taking on a similarly purposeful, assertive tone, "how come this line—" He pointed to the x'd out line that had read: **CVC: The Bigger Picture** "—was just crossed out? I mean, I know it had been a late night, and Fallon didn't get much sleep and all, but what could it take? Two, maybe three minutes to re-do it? And how much time did he have? Five, six hours? I mean, if Fallon was . . . what were the words you used, Ms. Thomas?"

"Fastidious? Compulsive?" Thomas replied.

"Yeah, that's it," Gatling said. "If Fallon was so fastidious— if he was so compulsive—don't it seem odd that he'd just cross out that line? Wouldn't he do it neater than that? Wouldn't he have re-done the agenda? Wouldn't he have taken the time to do it—What's that you all keep saying?—exactly right?"

"There's no way Michael Fallon would have just crossed a line out and scribbled in a change like that," Bill Tollikson said. "Not unless he had absolutely no choice in the matter."

"From what you all told me, I figured the same thing," Gatling said, nodding his head, scratching his chin. "Especially the way the agenda is printed in nice, block letters, but this line here—Opening Remarks—is written in, you know . . . what do you call this?"

"Cursive," Tollikson said.

"Yeah, thanks, cursive," Gatling continued. "Then it hit me—badda-bing, badda-boom—in the gut. Like I say, I can't explain it. It just works for me, that's all."

They all leaned in, eager—anxious—to hear just what the "it" was that had hit Gatling.

"What it was that hit me," he said, reading their minds, "was this: Fallon didn't cross out the line and scribble in the change, did he . . . Mr. C?" At once, all of the studied innocence from Gatling's tone was gone. Gone was the shambling aw-shucks manner. Gone was the disingenuous modesty. In its place was the granite assuredness of a man who had moved solidly through the sordid world of homicide for more than two decades.

Carpenter said nothing in response. Gatling didn't seem to care.

"Maybe what happened instead was this," Gatling continued, eyes now burning into Ronald Carpenter. Carpenter didn't—he couldn't—meet Gatling's gaze. "You got in late Sunday night. When you checked in, there was a package from Fallon waiting for you. It contained the memo about the Value Effect.

"You were tired. You started reading it, skimming it, but before you had gotten past the first few pages, you knew you had better do more than just skim it. This was way too important. This had— " He picked up Fallon's Value Effect memo and read: ". . . 'enormous strategic significance' for you.

"You read through the whole thing. Probably two, three times. That's why it was two o'clock before you knocked on Fallon's door. 'Cause Fallon's memo said some other pretty interesting things. Like this. Listen to what he has to say here: 'What's keeping change efforts from being successful isn't a shortage of tools and techniques. There are plenty of NBTs around today, and they are good things. Others will emerge as they are needed. That, too, is good. But it's not enough. What's missing are two key bits of the soft stuff: *context* in which to place them, and the *energy* to apply and sustain them. That brings me to the following statement: 'Skillful application of the Value Effect creates an energizing context for change.'"

Gatling paused momentarily, then pressed on.

"Now let me go back a bit. . . ." He flipped assuredly through the memo's pages. "Yeah, here it is. He's talking about how the soft stuff is going so well at Lodestar and how interesting it is that—and I'm quoting here: Listen carefully, 'cause this is important, 'I'm doing absolutely nothing different about the soft stuff than what I've ever done when working with a client to implement an NBT.'

"In other words, it just kinda happens. That's what the Value Effect is. Ain't that beautiful? In fact, listen here, let me read you some more: 'The beauty of it from Condor's perspective is that . . . . we don't have to develop a lot of snazzy new techniques and protocols before we can help clients apply it. We just have to help them understand how they can use the Value Effect to create an energizing context for change, how they can wring more out of the NBT investment they've already made, and how they can be more effective in using the Next Big Things that will invariably come along.'

"And look at what's here," Gatling said, holding up the first page of the memo for everyone to see. "There's a little handwritten note. What's it say here, Mr. C? What did Fallon write, right on the front?"

"'Ronald, this could be dynamite for us!'" Carpenter replied. He had never looked up. He hadn't had to.

Gatling dropped the memo onto the table—*thwackkk!*—directly in front of Carpenter.

"Michael Fallon," Gatling continued in bone-chillingly matter-of-fact tones, "saw the Value Effect as the thing that could finally help people deal more effectively with what he called—what *you* called—the soft stuff. He saw it as being very significant that the Value Effect was *not* an NBT, that people already had plenty of NBTs, that what they needed was context and energy to apply the NBTs they already had. He saw this as a huge opportunity.

"You don't see it that way at all, do you, Mr. Carpenter? In fact, you see it as a huge threat to you and everything you've built over the past fifteen years."

Carpenter struggled to maintain his customary studied serenity. Gatling continued.

"After all, you're in the NBT business," Gatling continued. "You've made a lot of money over the years by helping clients apply one NBT after another. That's what you do. That's who you are. Then along comes Fallon—your own guy—with some idea that there's a thing called the Value Effect that might change all that. That if it was understood and applied, people wouldn't need to keep looking so desperately for the next Next Big Thing . . . and then the next . . . and then the next. Or at least not as often. And even when a new NBT came along and they had to use it, they'd be better equipped to handle it on their own. They'd see how it fit into the bigger picture. They'd have a clear context to put it in. Things wouldn't seem quite as complex, so they wouldn't need as much consulting help. At least not the kind of consulting help you been providing for all these many years.

"If I'm reading this right, Fallon is saying that once you understand and apply this thing called the Value Effect, you have relatively less need for the kinds of things that consulting firms like Condor offer.

"So, when you went to Fallon's room at two o'clock, you were thinking that telling everybody else—telling *anybody else*—about the Value Effect wouldn't be such a hot idea. You tell Fallon that what he's written about the Value Effect is wonderful stuff. In fact, it's so wonderful you need more time to think it through so that you can do it justice when you talk about it. So, why don't you postpone your talk until Tuesday.

"But Fallon doesn't like that idea. He says that your talking about the Value Effect is the perfect way to start the two-day meeting . . . that if everybody has this information, it will be a much better meeting. Fallon could be a pretty persuasive guy. So, you said OK. Then you slept on it. Come to think of it, you probably didn't get much sleep, but you sure as hell thought about it some more. You still couldn't figure out exactly what to do. You needed to buy some time.

"So, you showed up in here—Meeting Room II—just before eight o'clock yesterday morning. You told Fallon that after thinking about it some more, you decided it would be best if you waited until Tuesday to talk about the Value Effect. Fallon pushed for Monday. You said that your decision was final. When Fallon started to argue some more, you got angry. You grabbed a marker, crossed out the line that said 'CVC: The Bigger Picture' and wrote in—in cursive, not in block letters—'Opening Remarks.'"

Gatling paused. Carpenter could still not meet his gaze. Gatling continued.

"As you sat through the meeting all day yesterday, it became clearer and clearer to you that Fallon was right about the Value Effect. Once you saw how energized everybody was, you understood its real power and potential. You knew that once everybody heard about it—even if it wasn't until Tuesday morning—that there would be no going back to the old way of doing things. No more coming out each year with a new Next Big Thing. And then the next Next Big Thing . . . and then the next . . . and the next . . . and the next. Fewer and fewer billable hours helping people with this or that set of tools and techniques . . . helping people sort through the complexity that results when there's no context for all the change that's going on.

"You realized that the Value Effect represented a threat to the very heart of your business. By the end of Monday's meeting, you also realized that what you had to do was clear. And so you did it."

Gatling looked down momentarily, leaving six sets of eyes burning into Condor's CEO. Carpenter met no one's gaze. Instead, he sat stoically in the screaming silence as Gatling approached and stood directly over him. He showed Carpenter the first page of Fallon's memo.

"What he wrote here: 'This could be dynamite for us, Ronald!' On one hand, that's another thing that Fallon got exactly right, isn't it, Mr. C?" Gatling said. "On the other hand . . . the *reason* it'd be dynamite for you . . . well, he got that part exactly wrong. And he paid for that mistake with his life."

Carpenter closed his eyes and took a deep breath. He started to speak. It was to no one in particular. And it was in anything but his strong, confident tones.

"Michael was like a son to me," he said. "Michael was . . . he was . . ."

"Yes," Gatling interrupted. "Michael *was*. And you made him that way."

Gatling gave an almost imperceptible nod to a uniformed police officer who had been standing in the doorway of The Wayne House's Meeting Room II. As the officer approached,

Carpenter meekly held out his wrists to the proffered handcuffs. Then he was led, slowly and silently, from the room.

After several moments, Bill Tollikson broke the pained, stunned silence.

"How did you know?" he asked Gatling, awkwardly. "I mean, I know you read the memo, but . . ."

"But I'm just a cop, right?" Gatling offered. "How could I see things so clearly? How could I understand the implications of what Fallon had discovered about the Value Effect if I'm not sophisticated about all this business stuff?"

Tollikson gave a small, apologetic nod.

"Good question," Gatling said. "I asked it myself. I'm sure Carpenter felt the same way. That's why he gave me the memo. Probably figured I would have found it before long anyway—and I would have—so, if he volunteered it, it would look completely innocent. So, he hands it to me—literally hands it to me—figures that way I won't be suspicious, that I'd pretty much ignore it. And, you know, he was right. Guys like Carpenter, nobody ever said they're not smart.

"Anyway, last night I finally got enough sense to read Fallon's memo, and you know what surprised me the most about it? That it was so clear and simple. The fact that I 'got it.'

"But, ya know, I *am* just a cop. I might *think* I got it, but I'm not *sure* I got it. You know what I mean? And you don't last twenty-two years in this business without being sure about being sure.

"That's why I read the quotes from the memo to all of you guys. It was a kind of test. If it didn't push any of your buttons, I would have figured I must have gotten things wrong. When I saw you all get so energized from what you heard—from just a few quotes read to you by an old gumshoe like me . . . well, that's when I knew that I really did get it after all. That was the last piece that clicked into place.

"That and the fact that Carpenter kept asking me whether any of you had heard of the Value Effect. Why would he do that? It didn't fit . . . didn't make sense . . . unless what he was doing was checking. Checking to see if anybody else was out there who knew anything about the Value Effect and could follow it back to him. Basically he had me out there checking for him to see if all of his tracks were covered."

"Very smart," Hatfield said, admiringly.

"Yeah, he's a smart guy, all right," Gatling said. "But, then ya know, Mr. Hatfield, there's lotsa smart people in the world. Sometimes they're just a little bit too smart for their own good."

More silence. Then Bill Tollikson stood and approached Gatling at the front of the room. For just an instant, it looked like he might give the detective a hug. Gatling gave a slight shiver, then he held out his right hand.

Tollikson took it, warmly, respectfully. Then he turned to his colleagues and said quietly, "I don't know about the rest of you, but I for one would like to get out of here."

There was no disagreeement.

"Why don't we all take the rest of the day off and compose ourselves the best we can. Let's meet tomorrow, eight o'clock sharp, back at the office. Figure out where we go from here."

They began silently gathering up their papers, portfolios, and briefcases.

Then Tollikson had another thought.

"Lieutenant Gatling," he said.

"Sir?"

"You have obviously gotten a good grasp of this thing that Michael called the Value Effect. You could," he added with a wan smile, "add a lot of value to our meeting tomorrow. Would you care to join us?"

Gatling gave a small nod of thanks.

"That's very nice, very flattering," he said. "But what do I know. I ain't a businessman. I'm a cop. Homicide. I cross names off a list. When there's just one name left on the list, I'm done."

And with that, Leonard H. Gatling, twenty-two-year-veteran homicide detective—be twenty-three years in June—turned and walked from Meeting Room II of The Wayne House, closing the door, and another case, behind him.

the evidence

Case: Fallon Homicide

Case No.: MPD-478-A-83

Lead: Gatling

WHILE YOU WERE OUT

TO: GATLING

FROM: CALLAHAN

TIME: 9:38 PM

MESSAGE:

LENNY—
PRELIMINARY
FORENSICS S/B
IN BY 10:00PM
— PAT

M.P.D. INTERROGATION LOG

Case No: MPD 478

The Wayne House

SU   TIME

R.   8 pm

T.   17 pm

B.   7 pm

C.   22 pm

S.   7 pm

D. H   4

B. To   56

Meeting Room II
Wayne House

EASER   SCREEN   EASEL   Door

EASEL

STORAGE TABLE   PROJECTOR   TABLE

VICTIM BOUND & GAGGED

MF   RC   BT   JS   BB   TM   CT   DH

Door

COFFEE

M.P.D. INTERROGATION LOG

Case No: **MPD-478-A-83**
Date: **11/15/99**

SUBJECT NAME	INTERROGATOR	BEGIN TIME	END TIME
D. Lee	Gatling	7:25 pm	7:58 pm
R. Carpenter	"	8:04 pm	8:47 pm
T. Magliori	"	8:52 pm	9:17 pm
B. Bradford	"	9:46 pm	10:22 pm
C. Thomas	"	10:42 pm	11:17 pm
S. Salinsky	"	11:38 pm	12:04 a.m.
D. Hatfield	"	12:26 am	12:56 am.
B. Tollikson	"	1:22 am	1:41 AM

Condor Group

INTEROFFICE MEMORANDUM

FROM: Michael Fallon
TO: Ronald Carpenter
SUBJECT: THE VALUE EFFECT
DATE: November 14, 1999

*Ronald,
This could
be dynamite
for us!*

Ronald, sorry to drop this on you at the last minute. I realize that you're probably reading this late Sunday night--maybe even early Monday morning, depending on how your connections worked out. (From your voice mail message the other day, it sounded like you had the itinerary from hell. Thanks for making the extra effort to get here.) I know that the last thing you need is a lengthy memo for your bedtime reading.

I hope you know me well enough to know that I would do this to you only if the matter at hand was both important and urgent, and I think I'm on to something that passes both those tests. If I'm right, it could have profound strategic implications for the firm; it's that important. What makes this so urgent is the fact that at 8:15 tomorrow morning, you're on the hook to make a presentation to the Lodestar executives. And if you think there's anything to what I've written here, you might want to share some of this with them at that time.

Page 1

Case No. MPD-478-A-83

We start at 8:00 Monday morning in Meeting Room II. How about if you and I meet in that room at 7:00 to discuss how--or even whether--you might want to talk about anything from this memo in your 8:15 remarks? Does that work for you? (There will be a continental breakfast set up in the room, so at least that's one thing you don't have to sweat.)

Again, my apologies for throwing you this curve, Ron. See you bright and early tomorrow morning. (Or later this morning, as the case may be.)

THE BACKGROUND

As you know, CVC has been going quite well at Lodestar. The strategy of getting everybody in the company not only connected *to* the customer but also deeply engaged *with* the customer in value conversations is clearly working.

We're seeing it in hard, business results: productivity up, efficiency up, time-to-market down. And we're seeing it in the kinds of insights that have emerged from the CVC teams, such as the singular importance of "dependability" to Lodestar's customers and the sales leverage they're getting from the new financing options they're offering to customers. You'll hear all about these and other examples during Monday's meeting.

Clearly the CVC tools and techniques that you initially came up with (and have since refined) continue to work beautifully. All of those things are rock solid--which only makes sense because they are, after all, the hard stuff.

As you've told me a thousand times, Ronald, "It's the soft stuff that's the hard part." And that brings me to the third most interesting thing I have to say in this memo: While implementing CVC at Lodestar, the soft stuff has gone better than it has with any other NBT implementation I've ever been involved with. (I have told you, haven't I, that NBT stands for "Next Big Thing"? That it's the term Lodestar uses to describe the various programs they've run over the past several years, like TQ and Empowerment and all the rest?)

Here's the second most interesting thing: I'm doing absolutely nothing different about the soft stuff than what I've ever done when working with a client to implement an NBT. And yet the results with the soft stuff--people's energy level, their focus, their enthusiasm--have been unprecedented. That unprecedented level of support will be formally ratified when Lodestar votes to continue CVC for a second year after Monday night's dinner. Guaranteed. (That's never happened with any other NBT at Lodestar.)

Case No. MPD-478-A-83

Conclusion: Something interesting is going on in the work we're doing at Lodestar, and it goes beyond the tools and techniques of CVC.

Which brings me to the most interesting thing I'll say in this memo: I think I understand what that "something" is. It's a phenomenon that--because you have to give these sorts of things a name--I will call "the Value Effect."

Here's a statement of the Value Effect:

*"When people strive to deliver
the maximum value to customers,
they get--and stay--energized."*

That's it. Just a simple, declarative sentence. It's not fancy. It's not complicated.

Here's another thing that it's not: it's *not* a Next Big Thing. NBTs are sets of tools and techniques and specialized expertise that help an organization deal more effectively with whatever is the issue of the day. The Value Effect, on the other hand, simply "is." It's a fact of human nature. It's a naturally occurring phenomenon, like water flowing downhill, or opposite poles of a magnet attracting, or ice melting when the temperature gets above 32 degrees.

It's been there all along; we just haven't seen it. That's not surprising, because we tend to see the world through NBT frames. After all, we're in the NBT business. Our stock in trade is tools and techniques, prescriptions and action steps and how-to's.

But if we only see what's been happening at Lodestar through an NBT frame, we will take what we've learned about CVC at Lodestar, we will successfully implement it with other clients, and we will make a very good buck in the process. That will be a damn shame, because the opportunity to make a real breakthrough with the soft stuff--the hard part--will blow right past us. Worst of all, we won't even know that we missed it.

To take full advantage of the Value Effect, we first have to see it, and for us to be able to see it, we have to look at things through new--or at least different--frames.

Consider yourself warned. On the pages that follow, I'm going to frustrate the hell out of you. I'm not going to go directly to the how-to's. Instead, I'm going to spend some time thinking and mulling on paper. Bear with it, and I think you'll see how gaining an understanding of the Value Effect could be of enormous practical value for our clients and, therefore, have enormous strategic significance for us.

THE PROBLEM ISN'T NEXT BIG THINGS. IT'S NEXT BIG THING-ISM.

How does a Next Big Thing emerge? I think it goes something like this: An issue arises in an organization. People have to deal with it. Generally, they can handle it themselves. Sometimes, though, they have to go outside for help. They have to bring in consultants. (Or they might create a cadre of internal consultants, which is just a private label version of the same thing.)

If enough different organizations have the same (or at least a similar) issue, this begins to constitute a market for consulting services. Consultants being consultants, they will "write it up" for a magazine or a journal, maybe even a book. More people hear about this hot new approach. They try it out. Get on board. There's nothing particularly remarkable about any of this. It happens all the time.

In a few cases, though, things play out a bit differently. When an issue is big enough, and when enough people have enough success in applying the hot new approach to dealing with it, a critical point is reached . . . and that's the point at which *the fact that a lot of people are applying an approach becomes reason enough for others to apply it.*

It's important to understand that this is most decidedly *not* a kind of mindless, monkey-see-monkey-do behavior on the part of organizations and their leaders. Under such circumstances, going along with the crowd is not only a defensible position to take; it's an essential one. That's because business success turns on the ability to attain relative advantage. It's not so much that you need to reach some sort of absolute level of perfection; it's that you need to be "better than the other guys." And in a world of relative advantage, if the competition is getting an edge by applying some "hot new approach," you have to respond. You have to close the gap. You have to apply the hot new approach too. (Think about the Quality movement. The principles of Quality had existed forever. The tools to apply them had been around for decades, but nobody used them. Until somebody did. The rest, as they say, is history.)

An approach becomes a certifiable Next Big Thing when the fact of some people applying it becomes a necessary and sufficient reason for others to do so as well. A second wave of consultants comes onto the scene to satisfy the demand for NBT services. More articles appear. More papers. More books. Whole new conferences are dedicated to this next Next Big Thing. Still more people get on board. Another wave of consultants. Still more papers and books.

Page 7

And so it goes, until we get to what is at
the real crux of the matter for us. The very same
thing that makes a Next Big Thing so essential for
an organization to apply will eventually cause it
to disappoint many (most?) of the organizations
that apply it. Why? Because in a world of relative
advantage, if *everybody* is doing something, then
that something *can't* provide a relative advantage.
Some organizations--the early adopters; the ones
who get written about by the consultants--get an
edge from the NBT. (Even that edge will be a
temporary one. Lodestar is in that position with
CVC right now.) For most of the others, though,
the reality doesn't live up to the rhetoric.

And it gets worse. Organizations are not made
up of automatons. They comprise flesh and blood
creatures with moods and emotions and all the rest
(you know: some of that soft stuff). When an NBT
falls short of its promise--"But I thought this
was supposed to be *the* answer?!"--people get
disappointed. And then another NBT comes along,
and a lot of people get disappointed again. As
these people make more passes through more cycles
of NBTs--as they engage in what might be thought
of as "Next Big Thing-ism"--that disappointment
becomes frustration, which eventually decays into
the kind of cynicism embodied in references to
"the program du jour" and "the flavor of the
month," or in the world-weary advice given to

the naively enthusiastic: "Don't worry. This too shall pass."

And because cynicism sucks energy out of an organization, later NBTs are even less likely to be effective, which breeds still more cynicism, still more frantic attempts to find the *next* Next Big Thing, and this cycle of NBT—ism--an especially vicious, pernicious cycle--continues.

Let me take a slight detour to address an important point. Over the years, Next Big Things have taken a bad rap. NBTs, properly understood and applied, tend to work just fine; that's how they get to be NBTs.

Again, take Total Quality. If you faithfully and correctly apply the principles and tools of Total Quality, you *will* have an organization that makes fewer mistakes, and your organization will, therefore, realize the improvements in efficiency and productivity that go with such reduced defect rates.

Well-designed, well-implemented Reengineering efforts *will* result in work processes that are more agile and nimble.

The principles of Empowerment, correctly understood and faithfully applied, *will* lead to a workforce that is more ready and able to step up to the challenges of the day. And without a well-honed Customer Focus, you can get so caught up in

internal work processes that your organization
might implode. (It will in all likelihood,
however, be a very efficient implosion.)

   More often than not, the "failure" of an NBT
is less a matter of its failing to live up to what
the NBT was initially designed to do and more a
matter of its failing to live up to expectations,
however unrealistic those expectations might have
been. A lot of the criticism of any given NBT is
less a matter of clear-eyed business analysis and
more one of petulance at a world that is not
sufficiently participating in our pipe dreams.
(You might want me to win the Kentucky Derby, and
you might expect me to win the Kentucky Derby, but
that doesn't make me Secretariat.)

   Of course, I also probably ought to acknowl-
edge the possibility that we in the consulting
trades might have had something to do with expectations getting a tad out of whack. ("What?! A
consulting company might have oversold its capa-
bilities? I'm shocked--*shocked!*")

   It's easy to blame clients for being unrealistic and consultants for being overly, well,
"enthusiastic." I think the world is a more complicated place than that. I think most clients are
doing their best at trying to sort through difficult jobs, and most consultants are doing their
best at trying to help clients sort through them.

So, we've got good, well-intentioned people, working hard, seeking the best answers and solutions for a very complicated world. I also think that these good, well-intentioned people understand and accept that change, and the pain that goes with it, is part of the job. (As has been said, that's why they call it "work.")

For the most part, I don't think that people are saying that they want everything to stay the same. They know that can't happen. What they're expressing--what they're feeling--is a need to have *something* stay the same . . . *something* stay consistent . . . *something* provide a frame of reference within which all of that change might make a bit more sense. A way of looking at things that is consistent and clarifying. In a word, *context.*

People also know that change is, as the saying goes, "a way of life." It will, in fact, never end. It will require perseverance, commitment, and a certain doggedness. To keep at it will take energy.

What's keeping change efforts from being successful isn't a shortage of tools and techniques. There are plenty of NBTs around today, and they are good things. Others will emerge as they are needed. That, too, is good, but it's not enough. What's missing are two key bits of the soft stuff: *context* in which to place them, and the *energy* to apply and sustain them.

Page 11

That brings me to the following statement:

Skillful application of the Value Effect creates an energizing context for change.

Again, nothing fancy or complicated. Just a simple, declarative sentence that, unless I miss my guess, suggests what might be thought of as an antidote for Next Big Thing—ism--and that suggests an enormous opportunity for us.

[ASIDE: From this point forward, Ronald, this document probably reads more like a "paper" than a "memo." Sorry for bouncing you back and forth between modes, but I wanted to get these thoughts in front of you prior to tomorrow's meeting, and this seemed to be the most direct way to do it. (It kills me to give you something that's not exactly right, but the clock is ticking!)]

VALUE: THE BASICS

Before you can effectively apply the Value Effect, there are some basics that need to be understood. Briefly, they are these:

▶ Customers buy on value . . . and only on value.

When all is said and done, the Value Effect is based on the premise that "value received" is the determining factor when customers hand over their money. Understand that I'm not saying that "value is one of the criteria by which customers make purchase decisions" or that "value is a critical consideration for customers." I'm saying something a lot stronger than that. I'm saying that customers buy on value and *only* on value. I'm saying that "to maximize value received" is the *only* reason that any customer in any industry has ever bought any product or service at any time. Ever.

▶ Value = GOT/COST

If I'm going to make that kind of categorical statement about the singular importance of value, then I have to have a definition of value to back it up. Here it is:

$$\text{VALUE} = \text{What-the-Customer-GOT/What-It-COST-the-Customer}$$

Or . . .

$$\text{VALUE} = \text{GOT/COST}$$

In this definition, GOT includes "product," plus "service," plus a whole host of intangibles. COST includes "money," plus "time," plus "sweat and toil," plus its own list of intangibles.

So, yes, when you buy a new car, you're getting (that is, your list of GOTs includes) a means of transportation, the various comfort and safety features incorporated within it, an extended warranty plan, and so on. And your COSTs include the purchase price, the time and effort it took shopping for the car, the dollar cost

involved in bringing it in for service and maintenance, and so forth.

   A less obvious GOT, however, might be the
head-turning reaction you want to induce when you
pull the new car into your driveway, or the peace
of mind afforded by the warranty coverage. An
additional COST could be the vague sense of guilt
you feel as a result of having bought your first
"import" or the overall anxiety you felt when
faced with the whole new-car-buying experience:
"Oh my God! I have to go back into the belly of
the beast!" Though intangible, such factors are
very real and are factored into customers' buying
calculations . . . into their value equations. It
may be at a subconscious level, but they're there,
and they're important. Exactly what makes up those
GOTs and COSTs will change over time, but what
doesn't change is this: Customers will go to
wherever their GOT/COST ratio is the highest.*

▶ Customer means customer.

Let's be clear about another definition. When I
talk about customers, what I mean is . . .
customers, people who pay money for goods and/or

---

*Just to anticipate an objection: You may be thinking, "Sure, you
can gain an edge by giving customers more and more product features
and gold-plated service. At some point, however, all of those extras
are going to wind up costing too much, and customers are not going
to be willing to pay for them." And that's true. That's why COST is
in the denominator; the value equation explicitly accounts for this
"too-muchness."

services. What I am *not* talking about here is the
so-called "internal customer." For the record, the
concept of the internal customer is a useful one
insofar as it can help get people to look beyond
the ends of their noses and recognize that they
are part of a larger work process. Without
question, it can help make a given process more
efficient and productive, but it begs the larger
question of whether it's the optimum process in
the first place. It's great if an HR department is
very efficient at screening new job applicants and
scheduling interviews with the hiring manager
(that is, HR's internal customer). Wouldn't it be
even better if HR could also drive the development
of job descriptions and identify the core competencies required to do that job based on a solid
understanding of what constitutes real value for
real customers? And don't you think that people in
HR would be more energized by this task than by
solely performing administrative duties?

Of course, the folks in the Systems department need to ensure that what they do serves the
needs of their colleagues throughout the rest of
the organization, but wouldn't it be better still
if all of that Systems work were done--consciously
and explicitly--as a means of maximizing the level
of value delivered to (real) customers? Wouldn't
that challenge engage the folks in Systems more,
and more deeply?

Case No. MPD-478-A-83

The (indisputable) fact that some people have a harder time than others in seeing the effects of their work on the customer shouldn't be seen as an excuse for rationalizing the difficulty away by telling them, "Your job is to serve your internal customer." It should be seen, instead, as an argument for looking harder and digging deeper to find everybody's connection to and effect on *real* customers. Those connections are there, and they matter a lot.

▶ The dynamic of value never changes.

Understanding value begins with an understanding of customer expectations. And here I'm talking about customer expectations for the entire buying and ownership experience, the entire service experience. Yes, it's essential to analyze and understand all of the complex, interrelated factors that go into those customer experiences. In fact, organizations tend to be pretty good at this already. What they're less good at, however, is keeping in mind the fact that customers "net out" their value considerations . . . that customers' GOT/COST calculations are for the *overall* experience, including the intangibles-- especially the intangibles.

Take a look at the following value scale.

The Value Scale

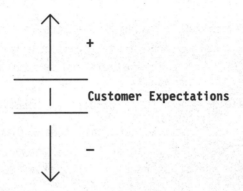

You'll notice that the scale has no upper or lower limit, that the arrows extend up and down indefinitely. What this is meant to convey is that absolute levels of value will vary dramatically over time, but what will *not* vary--what enables a focus on value to provide a steady, consistent context--is the fact that all of the action revolves around customer expectations (or as the economists like to say, "All interesting things happen at the margin").

An example from (fairly) recent history. Twenty-five years ago, the average new car manufactured in this country had something on the order of six to eight defects when it was delivered to the customer, who would then have to make,

Page 17

on average, two or three trips in for warranty
service during the first three months of new
car ownership.

When people bought those cars, did they
receive value? Absolutely. The car they GOT and
the COST they paid--defects and service trips
included--combined to give them a level of value
that fell within their band of expectations.

Would the same cars sell today? Of course
not. Why not? Because such performance would put
them in the minus range on the Value Scale. Value
is an inherently relative property. It depends not
only on what you have to offer, but on what you
have to offer relative to the other alternatives
open to the customer. When people buy cars today,
they expect virtually no defects and no un-
scheduled service trips.

Consider a hypothetical example of more
recent vintage. Suppose you ran a bookstore.
Business is great. Customers are happy. You've got
the sales and satisfaction scores to prove it.
Then one day a "dot-com" alternative appears, and
your sales go down. In an absolute sense your
performance hasn't changed at all, but what makes
customers buy is value, and value is a relative
proposition. The dot-com alternative caused
customer expectations for what's involved in
buying a book to change. Customers recalibrate

their Value Scales. The expectations line moves
up. You now fall in the minus range. Sales go down.

What makes this important in a discussion of
the Value Effect is this: The seemingly unremit-
ting change of today's world can be more than a
little daunting and unsettling for people. The
fact that the fundamental dynamic of value does
not change--it always has been and always will be
about where you fall on the Value Scale as shown
on page 17--can provide a solid and reassuring
context for understanding and dealing with all of
that change. It enables you to point at that Value
Scale and say, "*This* is what we're dealing with.
This is what we must understand and focus on. That
will *never* change." Knowing this--being able to
count on *something*--is steadying and reassuring
for people. Soft stuff.

▶ Value is personal.

The intangible "head-turning reaction" I referred
to in the hypothetical new-car buyer example is
only a GOT if that particular new-car buyer cared
about making people's heads turn. The "Oh my God!
I have to go back into the belly of the beast!"
reaction to the prospect of shopping for a new car
is only a COST for customers who happen to suffer
from that particular phobia. Your bookstore might
fall into the minus range for those customers who
know exactly what book they want, can wait a

Case No. MPD-478-A-83

couple of days to get it, and don't want the
hassle (a COST) of having to make a trip to your
store. On the other hand, for a customer who has
to have the book today or who enjoys the experience of browsing in a real bookstore, the GOT/COST
calculations might well keep you safely at--or
above--the expectations band.

Value also depends on the circumstances in
which a person might find himself. Which represents greater value: Dinner at McDonald's? Or
dinner at the Ritz? Well, if what you want is a
quick bite to eat on the way to a movie matinee
with the family, then a quick pass through the
golden arches probably makes more sense. If, on
the other hand, you're looking for a suitable way
to celebrate a twenty-fifth wedding anniversary
(and you have a desire to celebrate a twenty-
sixth), then the Ritz is probably the better bet.

The point to be made here is that value is
personal, that is, it has to do with your customer
as a "person," not as an account number, or a
checkmark in one of the cells by which you've
segmented your markets, or as a dollar amount that
gets aggregated into your overall sales figures.
Consequently, you can't pretend to understand
value until you understand your customers: who
they are, what their world is like, what's
important to them, what their current circum-

stances are, how those circumstances might be changing, what alternatives are available to them, how aware they are of those alternatives, et cetera, et cetera, et cetera.

▶ Everybody has a lifetime's experience as a customer.

If there is a secret to the Value Effect, it's this: The fact that everybody in an organization has a lifetime of experience as a customer is an enormously powerful lever, and that lever tends to be dramatically underutilized.

People know--profoundly--what it means to be a customer. They know what pleases them and causes them to go back for more. They know what displeases them and causes them to seek out alternatives. Yet they get on the job, and they tend to lose sight of that fact and how it might relate to their work.

What organizations need to say to people is this: "Remember how delighted you were when your insurance agent followed up with you to make sure that the claim had been settled quickly when the pipe burst in your house? *That's* what we want our customers to feel!" And, "You know how angry and frustrated you were because it took you so much time and so many phone calls to get that billing snafu cleared up with the XYZ Company? *That's* what we've got to make sure our customers *don't* feel!"

Case No. MPD-478-A-83

And words such as *angry* and *delighted* and
frustrated and *feel* are exactly the right ones.
Remember, we're trying to get at the soft stuff.
The fact that everybody "gets it" about being a
customer--that shared "customerness"--is a lever
that can help us pry that experience base open
and get at the energy that's contained inside
those emotions.

WHY THE VALUE EFFECT WORKS ...
WHY FOCUSING ON CUSTOMER VALUE ENERGIZES PEOPLE.

▶ Because everybody understands it.

To say that "Our goal is to deliver the most value
possible to our customers" is simple and straightforward. There is nothing arcane about it. It
isn't couched in a lot of consultant-speak. It
makes sense on the face of it. It passes the
sniff test.

▶ Because everybody feels it.

When you talk about delivering customer value,
you're not only engaging people at an intellectual
level. You're engaging them viscerally, too. Why?
Because they've all been customers all their
lives. It squares with their experience at a gut
level. They know both the upset and the delight
that they can feel as a customer. There's energy
in those feelings. The challenge lies in finding

the resonant frequency that releases that
energy; saying that "Our challenge is to deliver
the most value we can to our customers" res-
onates with people.

*[Aside: Ron, I realize that on one page I say it's
a "lever," and then on the next page, I talk about
"resonant frequencies." I'm not sure I'm mixing
metaphors here as much as I seem to be collecting
them. Which one works the best for you?]*

▶ Because it puts everybody in the mainstream of
   the business.

People want to work on something important; it's
energizing to know that you are making a difference
on something that matters. In the final analysis:
(1) What matters in business is "getting customers
to choose us instead of the other guys"; (2) Customers buy on value; (3) Value is a function of the
entire purchase, ownership, and service experience;
and (4) *Everyone* has an effect on that.

   The problem is that too many organizations
say this: "Those of you who don't have 'real'
jobs--you know who you are: Human Resources,
Accounting, Systems, and all the rest of you who
represent pure overhead--you should think of the
person who receives your work as your customer.
If everyone serves their internal customers well,
then it stands to reason that our external customers will be happy, doesn't it?" As a matter of

Case No. MPD-478-A-83

fact, no, it doesn't. Here's the test: Would you
rather be a customer of a company that has people
focused on serving each other? Or one that has
everyone focused on delivering value to you?
Me too.

When you apply the Value Effect, people
aren't let off the hook. It forces the issue,
saying in effect: "It's hard for you to see how
what you do on the job affects our customers? Too
bad. Find it anyway." And you know what? The connections are there to be found. People want to
find them. They will find them. When they do, they
will say: "For the first time, I see that what I
do can make a difference!" And that realization
is energizing.

▶ Because it's positive.

Go back to the Value Scale. The goal is to be able
to perform in the positive range. Operationally,
that means figuring out how to perform so well
that you can drive up the expectations line for
your industry (that is, so that customers will
recalibrate their Value Scales). Over the long
haul, that is a lot more energizing for people
than focusing on eliminating problems and driving
out defects. (Please note that I didn't say it was
more "necessary" than dealing with problems and
defects. I said that was more "energizing."
Remember: The issue is the soft stuff.)

Page 24

▶ Because it's "other-focused."

People want to work to a higher purpose than
just pulling a paycheck or avoiding a pink slip.
Working to truly understand customers and the
world they live in, to truly understand what
represents real GOTs and COSTs to customers, to
truly understand how your organization can provide
products and services that are truly "of value" to
someone else . . . that meets this most basic--and
most human--of needs.

Let me take a moment here to make a subtle
but, I think, essential distinction. There's a
difference between being "customer-focused" and
being "other-focused." The term "Customer Focus"
is not a new one. (In fact, it's on most people's
lists of NBTs.) And the impulse to want to be more
customer-focused is perfectly sensible. In fact,
it's essential. Human nature being what it is,
there is always a tendency toward self-absorption
--being all wrapped up in one's own "stuff." By
extension, organizations suffer from the same
tendency. The emphasis in recent years on such
disciplines as Quality and Reengineering--
disciplines that require a deep knowledge and
mastery of internal work processes--can exacerbate
that tendency toward institutional self-
absorption. Many organizations have recognized
this problem and launched efforts to combat it:
"Yes, it's important for us to focus on our

Case No. MPD-478-A-83

internal work processes, but it's also important for us to pay attention to how those processes affect our customers. To that end, we need to adopt a sharper Customer Focus."

Perfectly sensible. Of course you need to know how what you do impacts your customers, but the typical approach to Customer Focus is still, paradoxically, highly self-absorbed. When an organization attempts to be more customer-focused, it generally involves going to customers and asking those customers to comment on the organization's performance. If it's an especially forward-looking organization, it might also ask customers about what it might be able to do in the future to serve them better, but the context for the discussion is still "us": what "we" are doing . . . how "we" are doing . . . what "we" might do in the future.*

A true understanding of value requires a different way of engaging customers. The conversation--and it should be exactly that: a conversation, not a survey or a questionnaire

---

*There's an old joke about a narcissist who is having dinner with some companions. During the dinner, he's dominating the conversation by talking about his favorite topic: himself. Eventually it dawns on him that his companions aren't exactly hanging on his every word. "Listen to me," he says, looking to make amends. "Hogging the discussion. Talking about myself. I should give somebody else a chance. Why don't *you* talk about me for a while?" The typical approach to Customer Focus could be said to manifest a kind of "institutional narcissism."

or some other rote, analytic means of engagement--needs to be about "them," not about "us." About "their" world, not "ours."

The difference ultimately comes down to a difference in prepositions: focusing "as" the customer, not just "on" the customer . . . to be truly focused on "the other" as opposed to having "the other" focus on us. It is a subtle difference but it can yield results that are anything but subtle. It can cause people to understand the customer more deeply . . . to be more empathic. That gets people working to a higher purpose, and that releases energy.

▶ Because it's stabilizing and enduring.

Take another look at the Value Scale. Amid all of the change and chaos of the modern business world, it helps frame the issue; it leads one to four key questions about "the entire experience of doing business with us":

1. What do customers expect?

2. What is our performance relative to those expectations?

3. What shortfalls do we need to close?

4. What would represent going beyond expectations to create a value advantage?

Being able to put things in such a context is useful in and of itself. It makes the world less foggy, less chaotic, less random. As such, it lowers people's levels of fretting and anxiety, thereby reducing a kind of institutional friction loss and leaving them with more energy that can be applied to more productive work.

Moreover, it is a context that will not change. As was said previously, while the absolute level of performance necessary to meet customer expectations will vary with time, this fundamental dynamic--what goes on "at the margin", that is, just above and below the expectations line--is always where the action will be. The pursuit of value can provide a constant frame of reference ... an overarching context for change ... a context that will endure.

Before I end this section, let me be absolutely clear about one thing:

Although the skillful application of the Value Effect provides an energizing context for change, and although that context is absolutely necessary to achieve change, it is by no means sufficient!

Said another way, it's great that by applying the Value Effect you know the four key questions that you have to ask. But a fifth question remains: How do you *answer* those questions?

Well, you start by getting a handle on just what your customers' expectations are for what you should be doing and their feedback as to how you've been doing it (sounds similar to Customer Focus). You'll need to be able to do those things reliably and repeatably and efficiently (kind of reminiscent of Quality). It would be a good idea for you not to be doing anything you really don't need to do, so that you can be agile and nimble enough to react to the inevitable changes that will occur in customer expectations and the new demands that will go with them (hello, Reengineering). You'd better have an organization in place in which people have the insight, responsibility, authority, and confidence to take action; there just isn't time for them to wait for the "right" answer to come from on high in the organization (Empowerment, anyone?). And you'd better bring all of those empowered people into closer, more frequent contact with customers so that they can continue to have a broad and deep understanding of what is truly of value to those customers (do I hear CVC calling?).

In other words, you need to be able to apply the principles, tools, and techniques that come with having gained a degree of mastery of the litany of NBTs that are out there.

Let me say it one more time: The Value Effect is *not* a Next Big Thing nor does it obviate the

Case No. MPD-478-A-83

need for NBTs. It is a naturally occurring
phenomenon which, if properly understood and
applied, can provide a useful complement to the
roster of NBTs that an organization has at its
disposal . . . an energizing, enduring context in
which to place them and which will support them.

That's all the Value Effect is, but that is,
I think, quite a lot.

GUIDEPOSTS TO APPLYING THE VALUE EFFECT

By "guideposts" I mean areas or clusters of
activities to which attention must be paid if the
full potential of the Value Effect is to be
realized. As you read this section, it may occur
to you that these tools and techniques don't seem
to be all that new or terribly different from ones
you've used or at least heard about. That's
because they're not. That's a big part of what
makes the potential of the Value Effect so great:
the fact that while applying it, you're in
familiar territory. To a great extent, you've
already got much of what you need. And that
realization is energizing, in and of itself.

GUIDEPOST #1:
**Make Sure Everybody Sees Maximizing Customer Value
as the Superordinate Focus of the Organization.**

Yes, there are any number of things that would
seem to provide a useful, sensible focus for an

organization. Write a list of NBTs and you've got
a list of such possible focuses. That's part of
the problem. Everything seems to make sense, so
nothing makes sense anymore. People feel at sea.
Everything seems to be constantly up for grabs.
Not a good situation. Dispiriting. De-energizing.
You need to take a position, you need to pick one
and stick with it, and the one that you need to
pick is, "Maximizing the level of value we deliver
to our customers."

There are three main components to doing this.

▶ Communications component.

The idea of maximizing customer value must be a
theme that reverberates throughout the institutional conversation. It must be a part of formal
presentations and watercooler conversations. It
must appear in feature stories in the company
newsletter as well as in comments written in the
margins of interoffice memos. It must inform lines
of questioning in monthly staff meetings and in
daily cafeteria bull sessions.

The good news is that when you do this, you
don't feel like you're swimming upstream. First of
all, that's because it makes sense and feels right
to people. Second, people *like* talking about
customer value. It reaches them. It touches them.
It engages them.

▶ Management component.

"Maximizing customer value" has to be an explicit
part of policies, practices, processes, and
procedures. Where are the connections to customer
value in the planning process? In the budgeting
process? In the design of your systems? How does a
goal of maximimizing customer value inform the way
you organize? The way you recognize people? Reward
them? Do you recruit and hire people based on
customer value considerations? Do you train people
with a steely eye toward maximizing the level of
value they can help deliver? Are your key business
processes informed by a deep and broad understanding of their role in delivering value to customers?

   "Maximizing customer value" must be more than
a pleasant abstraction. To be blunt about it,
management has to drill it into the bones of the
organization. (Sorry about sounding harsh, but
life sometimes has sharp edges.)

▶ Leadership component.

Simply stated, leaders must ask themselves--
faithfully, diligently, resolutely, unflinchingly--
the same question they're asking everyone else to
face: "How does what I do affect the level of
value we are able to deliver to our customers?"
   Because the actions of leaders affect
"everything," this can get complicated.

Consequently, asking this question can be a tough
thing to do, the good news is that the Value
Effect will give leaders a firm push in the
direction of asking it. Why? Because the answer
gets at their two most fundamental issues: "What
is it that we need to do to get customers to
decide to give their money to us rather than to
the other guy?" And, second: "How can I get people
aligned and energized to make the changes
necessary to do it . . . to embrace change and
adopt an ethos of 'changing'?"

**GUIDEPOST #2:
Make Sure That Everybody Knows the Basics.**

They're listed here. They're discussed on pages
12 through 22. It's essential that everyone has a
handle on them.

- Customers buy on value and only on value.

- Value = GOT/COST.

- Customer means customer.

- The dynamic of value never changes.

- Value is personal.

- Everyone has a lifetime's experience as
  a customer.

Page 33

GUIDEPOST #3:
Make Sure That Everybody Knows Who the Customer Is.

The question of just who the customer is is a nontrivial one to answer. (And that's true even after you've gotten past the confusion that may have been caused by thinking in terms of "internal customers.")

Is it the distributor to whom we sell our products directly? The retailer who buys from the distributor? Or the consumer--the end-user of the product?

Is our customer the guest who stays at our hotel? The travel agent who points the guest in our direction? The meeting planner who is just as interested in our conference facilities as in our guest rooms?

Is the customer the chief financial officer who has to approve the expenditure? The plant manager? The operator on the factory floor who will use our product day to day? The mechanics who keep it up and running?

The point is not that the Value Effect magically reveals the answers. It doesn't, but it does make sure that the questions get asked. And can there be a more fundamental set of questions for an organization to address? The very act of joining the question will provide important insight as well as invaluable focus and alignment.

Now that you know who your customers are, what do you do next? There's no magic here, either. Once people understand who it is they're working to maximize value for, they need to be reminded . . . and then reminded again . . . and then again. How? You need to find ways to "make the customer come alive for all employees." By bringing customers in to your sites to meet with people face to face. By bringing people out to customers' sites. By running focus groups and showing videotapes of those focus groups to everyone. By interviewing customers on audio tape and providing tapes (or transcripts of the tapes) to everyone. By featuring customers prominently in company meetings, newsletters, and all other communications devices. (You may not have to create as many new mechanisms as you think. You might just have to be more opportunistic with the customer connections you're already making: Are you milking those connections for all they're worth?)

Once again, nothing tricky. Nothing particularly new. Just basic, probably familiar techniques applied from a slightly--but importantly--different perspective.

GUIDEPOST #4:
Make Sure Everybody Knows
What Is of Value to Customers.

Does everybody have a good understanding of the
world in which your customer lives? Can everybody
describe--using your customers' words, not your
company's jargon--just what it is that represents
value to them? Does everybody know what your
customers' GOTs are? Their COSTs? Can everybody
discuss--in the voice of the customer--just why it
was that they bought from you rather than from the
other guys?

[Aside: Ron, Ann Garber, one of the Lodestar
associates who will be presenting on Monday, has
a particularly "colorful" example of this. Be
listening for it.]

The single best way to make this happen is
to have everybody in the organization engaging
customers in conversation on a regular basis, and
when I say everybody, I mean everybody. Of course
it's important for Sales and Service and Marketing
people to have regular customer contact; that's at
the heart of their jobs. But it's also important
for "everyone else" to connect with customers.
People from Human Resources . . . Administration
. . . Systems Support . . . Accounting: all of the
traditionally non-customer-contact functions need

to make those connections. Otherwise, how are they to be aware of how what they do can affect the level of value delivered? How can they be expected to identify new and better ways to deliver value if they don't have that kind of contact? How can they be expected to truly "get it" about customer value.*

And when I say "conversation," I mean "conversation." What constitutes a conversation? An open exchange of information and affect. Genuine curiosity. Real interest in what the other has to say. This is different from (note: not a substitute for, but different from) the usual way in which organizations engage customers in communication. Usually it's done through surveys or interviews or focus groups. Usually, the line of discussion is around the performance of the business ("How are we doing?") or the potential performance of the business ("What *could* we be doing?"). Simply stated, the focus--the emphasis-- of such customer conversation should not be on "How are *we* doing?" but on "How are *you* doing?" instead. It should be aimed at helping you determine how you fit into your customer's world,

Case No. MPD-478-A-83

---

*As a practical matter, it may be impossible for everyone to participate in such conversations all the time. People still have their jobs to do, but representatives of everyone--all people, all functions --should be participating at any given time. Representation should rotate so that everyone--literally everyone--participates in such conversations periodically.

not the other way around. It's a subtle, but
powerful, difference.

GUIDEPOST #5:
Make Sure Everybody Is Actively and
Explicitly Engaged in Sustaining the
Level of Value Delivered to Customers.

Before you get fancy, make sure you've got the
basics covered. Before you try to operate in the
positive range of the Value Scale, make sure
you're not doing anything that will drive you down
into the negative range (and your customers into
the hands of the other guys). This is hard work,
requiring high degrees of diligence, discipline,
and attention to detail. There is absolutely
nothing glamorous about it.

An accurate (albeit slightly vulgar) way of
putting it is to say that the objective here is
"not screwing up." Because the superordinate goal
is customer value, and because customer value is a
function of the customer's entire experience of
doing business with you, and because everything
can affect that experience, then everybody needs
to pay attention to "not screwing up." Everybody
needs to understand how what they do on the job
can push you toward the minus range, and then they
must take whatever steps are required to ensure
that that doesn't happen.

That's one way to put it. Here's another way: "Our goal is to deliver the maximum value to our customers. An important part of doing that is to ensure that none of the value that we're all working so hard to create falls through the cracks before it can be delivered to our customers. Although our ultimate goal is to find new and creative ways to deliver customer value, before we do that, we need to make sure the foundation is solid. That's a responsibility we all share and an obligation we all have to our customers as well as to each other."

Once again, the *way* you make sure the foundation is solid is through the application of various NBTs. To know where the foundation begins, you need to know customer expectations, and Customer Focus will help with that. You need mastery over work process, and that puts you in the domain of Quality and Reengineering. You need everybody worrying about and able to deal with all of the above, that is, you need an Empowered work force. And you need everybody in closer, more frequent contact with customers; you need to Create Value Connections. But you also need to pay attention to how the change effort is positioned. It's a matter of saying to people: "This is why we're doing what we're doing. This is why it's important." This may seem like "just" a matter of

Case No. MPD-478-A-83

semantics, but semantics matter--especially when
you're dealing with the soft stuff.

GUIDEPOST #6:
Make Sure Everybody Is Actively and
Explicitly Engaged in Finding New Ways
to Deliver Value to Customers.

This *is* the part that's glamorous. This *is* the
part with sex appeal. People *do* like to be innovative and creative, they *do* like to take on the
challenge of not just "performing adequately" and
"not screwing up," but also of "rewriting the
rules" and "moving up the expectations line."

Everybody has an important part to play here.
Businesses have gotten pretty good in recent years
at mastering work processes. They've gotten pretty
good at maintaining a (traditional) customer
focus. The opportunity to come up with truly
innovative, breakthrough ways to deliver more
customer value may be the greatest of all in what
have traditionally been thought of as non-
customer-contact functions. Moreover, people from
such non-customer-contact functions bring fresh
sets of eyes to the task at hand. They may see
opportunities that traditional customer-contact
people do not--cannot--see.

[ASIDE: Ron, during tomorrow's meeting, listen
for the breakthrough idea that came from plant
management.]

Page 40

"Everybody" has their hands on the processes that might affect customer value. "Everybody" has a unique perspective to bring to the challenge of identifying opportunities for creating more customer value. And "everybody" gets psyched--energized--when they're given a chance to take part in that challenge. Find ways to make that happen.

GUIDEPOST #7:
Make Sure Everybody Is Conscious of and Explicit About the Application of "The Value Effect."

The Value Effect occurs naturally. That the pursuit of value energizes people is a fact of nature, not a Next Big Thing. There doesn't need to be--there *shouldn't* be--a lot of hoopla and razzmatazz associated with the application of the Value Effect. That's a good, refreshing thing.

The danger, though, is that because it occurs so naturally, it can be easy to forget that something called the Value Effect exists and can be put to use. Because it just sort of "happens," it can be easy to take for granted and overlook what it has to offer you. Remember: Even though the Value Effect just sort of happens to you while you're doing other things, that doesn't mean that effectively applying it is automatic. Tools and techniques *are* required. (Gravity just sort of "happens," but you wouldn't try to sky dive without a parachute and some training, would you?)

Case No. MPD-478-A-83

This guidepost is saying, simply, this: "Make sure that you explicitly remind yourself, at regular intervals, that something called 'the Value Effect' does indeed exist (that is, people are indeed energized when they focus on value) and that this effect can, if properly understood and consciously applied, help you achieve the kind of performance you're after." Be conscious of the competence you've attained; then it will be there, on your screen, when the time comes for you to use it again.

THE VALUE EFFECT

"When people strive to deliver the maximum
value to customers,
they get--and stay--energized."

The Strategy

Create an energizing context for change
by skillfully applying the Value Effect.

The Basics of Value

- Customers buy on value and only on value.
- Value = GOT/COST.
- Customer means customer.
- The dynamic of value never changes.
- Value is personal.
- Everyone has a lifetime's experience as a customer.

The Value Scale

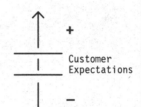

Customer
Expectations

Why Focusing on Customer Value Energizes People

- Everybody understands it.
- Everybody feels it.
- It puts everybody in the mainstream of the business.
- It's positive.
- It's stabilizing and enduring.

Guideposts to Applying the Value Effect

- Make sure everybody sees "maximizing customer value" as *the* superordinate focus.
- Make sure everybody knows the basics of value.
- Make sure everybody knows who the customer is.
- Make sure everybody knows what is of value to customers.
- Make sure everybody is actively and explicitly engaged in sustaining the level of value delivered to customers.
- Make sure everybody is actively and explicitly engaged in finding new ways to deliver value to customers.
- Make sure everybody is conscious of and explicit about applying the Value Effect.

Ron, thanks for wading through all of these ideas. (By the way, we're now back in "memo mode.") In the chart on the preceding page, I've tried to summarize the key points. By way of leaving you with a few closing thoughts, let me tell you a brief story.

Bill Tollikson and I have had a kind of running joke going over the last couple of months. He'll say to me: "CVC is going great. In fact, it seems to be going better than any other NBT we've tried." Then he'll invariably smile, shake his head, and say: "Sorry to burst your bubble, Michael, but I'll be damned if I understand why that is. Don't get me wrong. The steps we're taking to create stronger value connections-- getting more people more closely connected with customers more often--make perfect sense, but the specific things we're doing don't seem all that different from some things we've done with past NBTs . . . at least not different enough to account for the feeling I have that the results we're getting are a lot different . . . significantly better." Then he always concludes with this phrase: "It's just not logical."

What do I do when he says that? I do what consultants are supposed to do. I give him the answer. I say, "Of couse it's logical. Those value connections we've created have reduced the inertial load caused by well-intentioned but less

than optimally productive employees who are
focused on internal-to-the-organization matters
rather than matters important to your customers.
The act of Creating Value Connections has shaken
up the bureaucracy and reduced the waste and
inefficiency that goes with it, and the value
connections you've formed are also helping to get
mission critical information to where it can do
the most good the quickest. What could be more
logical than all of that?" He'll listen, smile,
shake his head, and say, "Sorry, but it's just
not logical."

Eventually we agree to disagree, but it will
still nag at me. "He's a smart guy," I say to
myself. "Why isn't he getting it about what makes
CVC so powerful?" It's been a real mystery to me.

Then, just this morning, it finally hit me.
It's not that *he's* not getting it. It's that *I'm*
not getting it! Why does this smart guy keep
saying that it's not logical? Because it's *not*
logical. It's visceral. It's in the gut. You know:
the soft stuff.

Yes, we've helped Lodestar create some new
value connections in a hard, mechanical sense.
Yes, we've helped them create some mechanisms that
facilitate information flow. And that's all very
useful. Helpful. All very sensible, very analytical. All very logical.

But it turns out that we were also getting
people to connect with customers in a deeper, more
personal way. We were (serendipitously) getting
them to connect their own experiences as customers
with what they were hearing from Lodestar's
customers. We were getting them to connect with
their innate and profound understanding of the
fact that, "Yes, that's what it feels like to be a
customer. That is something that I not only
understand, but that I empathize with as well."
That empathy is packed with energy, and it's *those*
connections that have enabled that energy to flow
at Lodestar.

You'll see that energy flowing in Monday's
meeting. Watch the executives. Even more
important--and more exciting--watch Garber,
Bergen, and Paulson, the three Lodestar associates
who will be presenting. Listen to their voices.
Look at their eyes. When you do, you'll realize
that we've tapped into a deep, rich vein.

Those kinds of value connections--the
visceral kind--were there all along, ready to be
made. So, what insight did we stumble into? The
fact that once the right elements are put into
close enough proximity, those visceral connections
will make themselves. *That's* what's been happening
at Lodestar. *That's* the Value Effect.

Don't get me wrong. The effective application
of the tools and techniques of CVC--the ones you
invented--represent a powerful and important
service that we can provide for our client. They
clearly deliver value. It's my guess that CVC will
be an NBT around Lodestar for the foreseeable
future, and that's great.

Even after CVC has become a past Next Big
Thing, though--still useful, still powerful, but
no longer the sexy new kid on the block--the Value
Effect will still be there. The beauty of it from
Condor's perspective is that because it's not an
NBT, we don't have to develop a lot of snazzy new
techniques and protocols before we can help
clients apply it. We just have to help them
understand how they can use the Value Effect to
create an energizing context for change, how they
can wring more out of the NBT investment they've
already made, and how they can be more effective
in using the next Next Big Thing that will
invariably come along.

Ronald, I know that I've got a lot more to do
to get ready for tomorrow, and I'm sure that you
do too. (If you think that there's some merit to
what you've read here, you may now have even more
work to do than you thought.) So, let me jump to
my bottom line:

Case No. MPD-478-A-83

I think helping clients understand and apply the Value Effect could represent a huge opportunity for Condor. What's your take? Let's discuss at 7:00 Monday morning.

About the Author

Named one of the "New Quality Gurus" by *Quality Digest* magazine, John Guaspari has been one of the business world's thought leaders for the past two decades on the topics of customer value, quality, and driving organizational change efforts by creating broader and deeper customer connections.

After thirteen years in the automotive and electronics industries, Guaspari turned to consulting in 1986. Since then he has worked in a broad range of industries helping hundreds of client companies apply the Value Effect. Today he is a co-founder of Guaspari & Salz, Inc., a Concord, Massachusetts–based management consulting firm.

John is the author of four previous books (including *I Know It When I See It* and *The Customer Connection*) and six video-based training programs (including *Why Quality?*, *Time: The Next Dimension of Quality,* and *The Force of Value*). He has written dozens of articles for such publications as *Management Review* and *The Journal for Quality and Participation.* His monthly column, "Dispatches from the Front," appears in *Across the Board,* the flagship magazine of The Conference Board.

Guaspari is a popular speaker for the American Management Association, The Conference Board, the Association for Quality and Participation, and hundreds of corporate clients.

He lives in Walpole, Massachusetts with his wife Gail, his son Mike, and his daughter Joanna.